TO BEGIN THE WORLD OVER AGAIN

TO BEGIN THE WORLD OVER AGAIN

Lawrence of Arabia from Damascus to Baghdad

JOHN C. HULSMAN

palgrave
macmillan

TO BEGIN THE WORLD OVER AGAIN
Copyright © John C. Hulsman, 2009.

First published in 2009 by PALGRAVE MACMILLAN® in the U.S.—a
division of St. Martin's Press LLC, 175 Fifth Avenue, New York, NY 10010.

Where this book is distributed in the UK, Europe and the rest of the world,
this is by Palgrave Macmillan, a division of Macmillan Publishers Limited,
registered in England, company number 785998, of Houndmills, Basingstoke,
Hampshire RG21 6XS.

Palgrave Macmillan is the global academic imprint of the above companies
and has companies and representatives throughout the world.

Palgrave® and Macmillan® are registered trademarks in the United States, the
United Kingdom, Europe and other countries.

ISBN: 978-0-230-61742-1

Library of Congress Cataloging-in-Publication Data
Hulsman, John C., 1967–
    To begin the world over again : Lawrence of Arabia from Damascus to
Baghdad / John Hulsman.
        p.   cm.
    Includes bibliographical references and index.
    ISBN 0-230-61742-5
    1. Lawrence, T. E. (Thomas Edward), 1888–1935.   2. Lawrence, T. E.
(Thomas Edward), 1888–1935—Political and social views.   3. Soldiers—
Great Britain—Biography.   4. Great Britain. Army—Biography.
5. Middle East specialists—Biography.   6. Nation-building—Middle East—
History—20th century.   7. World War, 1914–1918—Middle East.
8. Great Britain—Foreign relations—Middle East.   9. Middle East—
Foreign relations—Great Britain.   10. Middle East—Politics and
government—1914–1945.   I. Title.
D568.4.L45H85   2009
941.083092—dc22
[B]

                                                              2009022873

A catalogue record of the book is available from the British Library.

Design by Letra Libre, Inc.

First edition: October 2009
10 9 8 7 6 5 4 3 2 1
Printed in the United States of America.

For my daughter Matilda, my Damascus

"We have it in our power to begin the world over again."

—Thomas Paine, *Common Sense*

Contents

Chronology

August 16, 1888	Lawrence is born in Tremodoc, Wales
1896	Family settles in Oxford
October 1907–June 1910	Attends Jesus College, Oxford
1911–1914	Helps run archaeological dig at Carchemish
August 1914	The Great War begins
December 1914–October 1916	With British Military Intelligence in Cairo
June 5, 1916	The Arab Revolt begins
October 16, 1916–October 1918	Fights with Feisal's legions in Arabia and Syria
October 23, 1916	First meeting with Feisal
May 9, 1917–July 6, 1917	Aqaba campaign
Spring 1918	Meeting with Lowell Thomas
September 19, 1918	Allenby launches final offensive for Damascus
October 1–4, 1918	Takes Damascus as the Arab cause is betrayed
January–September 1919	Versailles Peace Conference

August 1919	Lowell Thomas's show opens in London
July 24, 1920	French victory over Feisal at the Battle of Maysalun
February 1921–July 1922	In the Colonial Office with Churchill
March 1921	The Cairo Conference
August 1922–February 1935	Serves in the RAF and Royal Tank Corps
May 13, 1935	Motorcycle accident
May 19, 1935	Death due to severe brain injuries following a week in a coma

Today's Saudi Arabia. Courtesy of the University Libraries, The University of Texas at Austin.

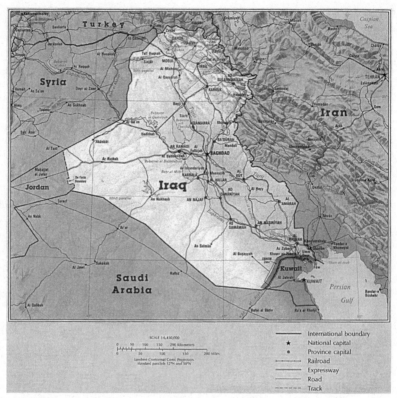

Today's Iraq. Courtesy of the University Libraries, The University of Texas at Austin.

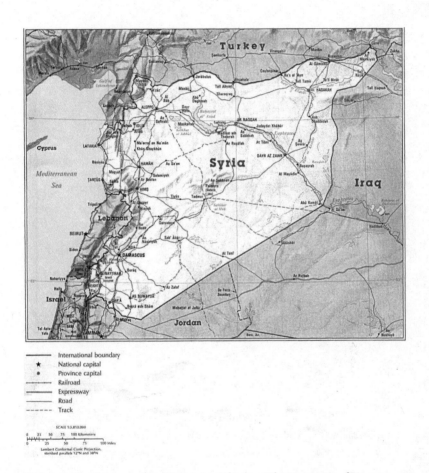

Today's Syria. Courtesy of the University Libraries, The University of Texas at Austin.

Prologue

"The story I have to tell is one of the most splendid ever given to a man for telling."

— T. E. Lawrence, letter to Vyvyan Richards

*J*ust before the start of the Iraq war and then again just after, the prestigious Council on Foreign Relations asked me to serve on two task forces. The aim of the first was to help advise the government on how to run Iraq immediately after the fall of Saddam. The second aspired to nothing less than devising a blueprint for creating stable countries from scratch. The Council was not alone in its ambitions. At the time it seemed that practically every think tank in Washington was doing the same thing; after the Iraq debacle, task forces on nation building were sprouting up everywhere. It was these experiences that drew me to Lawrence.

The meeting of the second task force opened with a presentation by another well-known think tank, grading America's recent efforts at nation building. By evaluating Somalia, Haiti, Bosnia, Kosovo, Afghanistan, and Iraq, the authors hoped to see which efforts had worked, which had not, and what best practices could be applied across the board for use in future nation-building initiatives.

They concluded, after painstaking analysis, that Kosovo was the jewel in the crown, the best example of successful nation building in the post–Cold War era. Supportive noises were made by the great and the good—not a word of dissent was uttered. And then we broke for lunch.

Not one critical word was raised questioning our "success" in Kosovo, where our allies, the ethnic Albanians, had just partially ethnically cleansed our erstwhile enemies, the Serbs. Of course, the whole reason we were there in the first place was that the Serbs, on a far larger scale, had earlier done the same thing to the ethnic Albanians. Yet, at the time, no one thought to mention this, or the fact that the key political problem underlying the ongoing Kosovo crisis—how to create a stable political entity in the country, in the face of the irreconcilable claims of the minority Serbs (Serbian national unity) and of the majority Albanians (Kosovo's national independence)—had yet to be seriously addressed. My colleagues seemed perfectly satisfied that American efforts at nation building were on the right track in Kosovo, despite quite significant evidence to the contrary. If this very ambiguous "success" is all modern nation builders have to point to, surely something is very wrong.

The second moment of blinding clarity occurred during the Iraq task force meeting. One of the points made over and over again was that, if nation building was to have a chance of success, inserting Western liberal democratic values into failed states as soon as possible was an absolute prerequisite. In the case of Iraq, it was suggested that embedding women's rights into both government institutions and civil society should be one of our immediate priorities. While such rights in general are certainly worthwhile, this attitude struck me as the height of lunacy.

I could visualize American governmental representatives soberly working their way through the teeming streets of Najaf, to meet with intermediaries of Grand Ayatollah Ali al-Sistani, the senior Shia cleric in Iraq and a man with an immense local following, earnestly telling him that, like it or not, he must support imposing a Western view of women's rights on his people, or else. Despite his reputation for saintliness, the Grand Ayatollah's response would not be printable. Forgotten in all this high-mindedness was the simple fact that, if we were ever to leave Iraq, we would need the Grand Ayatollah's help far more than he would need ours; this was probably not the ideal way to attain it.

Over the next hours of discussion, we proceeded to ignore Iraq's unique history, politics, culture, ethnology, sociology, economic structure, and religious orientation. What did these trifles matter, compared with our eminently reasonable view of how the world should work? Then, seemingly from nowhere, came something better, which encapsulated what was so horribly wrong with the common philosophy of all the nation-building experts in the room. These words came to me, and I spoke them aloud, without my knowing their origin, and without getting the quotation quite right. "Do not try to do too much with your own hands. Better the Arabs do it tolerably than you do it perfectly. It is their war, and you are to help them, not win it for them." To help them—not dictate to them, manage them, bully them, ignore them, or pontificate to them—to help them help themselves.

Fleetingly, this idea has been remembered, and in some very strange circumstances. On the day Saigon finally fell to the North at the end of the traumatic Vietnam War, English poet James Fenton found a similar sentiment framed on the wall of the ransacked American embassy: "Better to let them do it imperfectly than do it perfectly yourself, for it is their country, their war, and your time is short."[1] The West has been here before, but its memory is short.

It suddenly occurred to me that the failed attempts at nation building in Haiti, Somalia, Bosnia, Kosovo, Afghanistan, and Iraq were all related; in every case they were based on the same philosophically flawed worldview. I knew that the quotation I had just blurted out in the meeting was not original, though I had entirely forgotten that it comes from Lawrence of Arabia's "Twenty-Seven Articles," written in August 1917 as a guide to British officers serving in the Arab Revolt during World War I.[2] I looked up the quotation, and began to find the man. It has been a rewarding journey into the desert. For if conventional wisdom about nation building has proven almost uniformly wrong, there are answers out there, answers the new Obama administration and the Western world are in desperate need of rediscovering. We must go back in time to the early twentieth century, where an increasingly famous British subaltern is hastily scribbling some notes in the wastes of the Arabian Desert.

TO BEGIN THE WORLD OVER AGAIN

Chapter 1

"[I like it] well; but it is far from Damascus."

—Lawrence to Prince Feisal, on the occasion of their first
meeting, October 23, 1916, *Seven Pillars of Wisdom*.[1]

Thomas Edward Lawrence was born in Tremadoc, Wales, on August 16, 1888, the second of his unmarried parents' five sons. His father, Sir Thomas Chapman, was a wealthy Anglo-Irish landowner descended from the Elizabethan adventurer Sir Walter Raleigh. Trapped in a disastrous marriage with a cold and fanatically pious wife, in the mid-1880s Sir Thomas had run away with the nanny to his four daughters, Sarah Lawrence, giving up the rights to his estate to his brother in return for 20,000 pounds and a yearly annuity. Chapman's furious wife refused to divorce him, forcing the stain of illegitimacy on Chapman's second family. In an attempt to break with the past, Chapman took his lover's surname, although it was never legally adopted.

Given Victorian social mores, the family was forced to move around a good deal, always fearing that scandal was following just behind them. Finally, in 1896, they settled in Oxford for good, at No. 2 Polstead Road. Ned (as Thomas Edward was known in the family) always considered Oxford his family's home.

Even as a child, Ned was an eccentric. Small, muscular, perpetually fidgeting, he was delicately handsome, with startlingly beautiful blue eyes, a large, well-made head, and long eyelashes; he was almost pretty. He had the ability, which he retained all his life, to draw others to him while remaining beyond their grasp. Possessing a soft voice and a nervous smile, Lawrence was often described in school as being quiet, self-possessed beyond his years, and cheerful but difficult to know. He was not, in English terms, clubbable, preferring solitary activities such as cycling or walking, while disdaining the organized sport that was so central to the English ruling-class ethos of his time. Even as a child, Lawrence was never much of a team player.

At the risk of being overly Freudian, it may be said that a large measure of the Lawrence's youthful diffidence sprung from his never-ending emotional struggle with Sarah, who was the dominant influence, for both good and ill, on his childhood. Whereas his father was seen by outsiders as a nice but inconsequential man—a bearded, quiet, gentleman of leisure (the settlement had left the family comfortably off) and, like his son, a passionate cyclist and photographer—his mother inevitably provoked strong reactions in all who met her. Sarah was small and neat, with golden hair, the same electric blue eyes as her son, and a fixed, determined jaw. Like Thomas's wife, she was deeply religious. Although their life together was outwardly respectable, her guilt at her adultery with Chapman never entirely left her. While not well educated, she was intelligent and opinionated, ranging to downright bossy, yet capable also of great warmth and loyalty.

Sarah came to be a dominant influence in the lives of all her sons. She ran the family like a drill sergeant, dressing all the boys identically in what amounted to the family uniform—white-striped Breton jerseys. Sarah would lose two of her sons, Frank and Will, in World War I. Of the three sons who survived to adulthood, only the youngest, Arnold, married, escaping by coming to ignore her as best he could. Ned, the family rebel, directly confronted her, bearing the brunt of Sarah's corporal punishment. Like many Victorians of her time, she believed that to spare the rod spoiled the child; Ned was repeatedly beaten, whipped over the bare buttocks. Ned spent almost the whole of his life trying to elude her formidable control. It is from this battle that his famous unconcern for social convention grew, as it was a guiding principle of his mother's life.

There was a general consensus within the family that Ned was the most intelligent of the brothers, displaying a quick mind and an independent spirit from the beginning. He grew up a great reader, especially of history, archaeology, and medieval legends, which were to remain passions throughout his life.

The feudal past, in particular, particularly held sway over him. With his friend Charles Beeson, Ned made brass rubbings in the many churches lying in the English countryside near Oxford. The two boys combed the city for the remnants of an earlier eras, though to Lawrence's chagrin most of his finds tended to come from the nonfeudal sixteenth and seventeenth centuries. Still, his collection of coins, pottery, and glazed ware was significant enough to be accepted by Oxford University's famous Ashmolean Museum of Art and Archeology. There, Lawrence met a young archeologist named Leonard Woolley, who then worked at the museum as junior assistant keeper. At the time, little did either the archeologist or this rather eccentric boy realize that they would be partners in running an archeological dig in exotic Carchemish together.

As he grew older, Ned's fascination with castles and crusades came to dominate his free time. As a youth, he made eight cycling trips to France, covering many thousands of miles and visiting every twelfth-century French castle of note. E. M. Forster, the famous novelist who was a friend of the adult Lawrence, later saw in this obsession the defining quality of Lawrence's life, saying "The notion of a Crusade, of a body of men leaving one country to do noble deeds in another, possessed him."[2]

At the age of 17, Ned had a profound and mysterious personal crisis, possibly relating to the discovery of his illegitimacy and his outwardly respectable parents' sordid past, but more probably relating to the climax in the struggle between his carefully constructed world of intellectual escape and his domineering mother. Ned's name was put forward for a mathematics scholarship at Oxford. However, given his passion for the Middle Ages, he wanted to study history. Sarah pressed her son to accept a place at the most prestigious university in the land. Lawrence, feeling cornered, suddenly rebelled—he ran away to join the army.

It is likely that Lawrence became a gunner in the Royal Garrison artillery, stationed at St. Just in Cornwall. The rough treatment of the soldiers that he witnessed there, as well as the brutal violence within the ranks, frightened him; he soon let his father know of his location. As was accepted custom of the time, Thomas Lawrence bought his son out of his military obligation. Despite what Lawrence later said to his friend and biographer Basil Liddell Hart, his time in the army was not lengthy; the whole affair probably lasted only days, occurring sometime in February or March 1906. There is curious proof that the event actually took place. After his death, a painting by the noted English artist Henry Scott

Tuke was found among Lawrence's effects. It shows a young man, who looks a great deal like Lawrence, in a gunner's uniform.

Whatever the particulars of this wrenching event, it enabled Ned to definitively break from his mother's overweening influence. While he remained devoted on the surface, from that moment on Lawrence gained a certain independence from his family. To begin with, he was allowed to study history rather than mathematics. Ned also persuaded his parents to build him a small cottage at the bottom of the garden at No. 2 Polstead Road. It was equipped with a telephone to the house, a working fireplace, a bedroom, a study, and piped water. Throughout his college years, Lawrence spent the majority of his time here, rather than living among the other undergraduates. The cottage's physical distance from his family's house mirrored the hard-won psychological distance Lawrence had put between his ever-expanding intellectual world and the domineering presence of his mother. Long after, he would say that he found himself at the age of 17.

On October 12, 1907, Lawrence entered Jesus College, Oxford, to study history. A year later, as a further sign of independence, Lawrence threw off the shackles of his oppressive Christian upbringing. In an early example of Lawrence's subversive nature, and his sense of humor, he read a religious story by the disgraced, openly gay British playwright and novelist Oscar Wilde—and consequently lost his long-running job as a Sunday school teacher. Wilde had gone to jail over a scandal involving his homosexuality, shocking Edwardian Britain. Thus ended Lawrence's career as a Christian.

That same year, to everyone's surprise, Lawrence finally joined a club. He became a cadet in the Oxford University Officer Training Corps, where he proved himself to be a good shot. He seems to have been able to set aside his horror of organizations because the Jesus College cadet contingent was a bike-mounted signals unit, meaning Lawrence could pursue his beloved cycling and spend as much time outdoors as possible.

Meanwhile, Lawrence's passionate enthusiasm for medieval epics continued to flower with his reading of Malory's *Morte d'Arthur* and Tennyson's collection of Arthurian legends, *The Idylls of the King.* Both books would remain lifelong favorites; the warrior Lawrence read Malory over and over again during the Arab Revolt.

This further intellectual grounding in tales of crusades and knightly feats of chivalry led Lawrence to his choice of a thesis topic. Among medieval scholars there had been a long-running academic dispute as to whether the Crusaders from the West had inspired architectural innovations in Eastern castles, or rather that, bedazzled by the forts of the East, they had brought Eastern architectural styles back to Europe. Lawrence, already an expert in Western castle architecture, proposed to study a large group of Eastern castles first-hand, in order to determine whether the pointed arch and vault originated in Europe or the Middle East.

But it was his proposed odyssey for determining this rather obscure point that was the real object of the whole undertaking. So, in 1909, at just 20 years old, Lawrence embarked upon a journey that few if any undergraduates would now be permitted to undertake through modern-day Lebanon, Palestine, and Syria. Traveling alone and principally on foot, he covered more than 1,100 miles in 83 days, at the height of the

Levantine summer. During the journey he contracted malaria (of which he experienced recurrences throughout his adult life) and seems to have been shot at and attacked by bandits. In spite of these perils, Lawrence visited three dozen or so castles (not 60, as he later claimed), drawing detailed sketches of their architectural features. Critically for his future, Lawrence learned rudimentary Arabic and about the local peoples, their customs, social and political conditions, and tribal structures.

Lawrence's thesis—that Western ideas of architecture had been adopted by the East—earned him a rare first-class degree in 1910. He was feted for his significant academic success by his tutor, Reginald Lane Poole, at a celebratory dinner, and tales of his undergraduate trip became the stuff of Oxford legend.

Lawrence's work on his thesis had brought him into contact with David Hogarth, the renowned British archeologist. At age 45, Hogarth had already lived the sort of life Lawrence aspired to. He had traveled alone through much of the Near East, including today's Syria, Turkey, and Palestine and had led archeological excavations in Cyprus and Egypt. Fluent in French, German, Italian, Turkish, and Greek, Hogarth was as superbly educated as he was adventurous.

Hogarth was a man of the mind, but he was also a man of the world. Sitting on the board of the Royal Geographic Society, Hogarth was well connected with the rulers of the British Empire in London. Indeed, if one were describing the standard Edwardian gentleman-imperialist, Hogarth would have done nicely as a model. Like a character in a Galsworthy novel, he was worldly, civilized, shrewd, conservative, and elitist. If Hogarth had a failing it was that while his talents were many, he never managed to concentrate on any one aspect of his career long enough to achieve genuine greatness. He is best known today as the man who discovered the young Lawrence. Years later, Lawrence admitted that that he owed to Hogarth every good job he ever had and that everything he had accomplished was due to him.

Before his undergraduate journey, Hogarth had set Lawrence an Arthurian task; to return from Syria with ancient Hittite seals that had piqued the archeologist's interest. Lawrence brought back 30 of the rare artifacts. Impressed with this obviously unusual young man, Hogarth offered Lawrence a job working on an archeological dig at the ancient city of Carchemish, a Hittite ruin located on today's Syrian-Turkish border. A Hittite provincial capital dating from as early as 2500 B.C., Carchemish had been discovered by the modern world in 1876. Mentioned in the Book of Jeremiah in the Old Testament, it overlooked the Euphrates River, giving it strategic importance in the ancient world. Hogarth was on the elusive trail of a word key that might uncover the ancient Hittite language, much as the Rosetta stone had done for the ancient Egyptian language of the Pharaohs. Hogarth wanted to excavate there to uncover the secret of Hittite hieroglyphics for the British Museum.

Hogarth saw to it that Lawrence received a scholarship from Magdalen College in Oxford in the amount of 100 pounds a year. This allowed him to continue his studies in the wider world.

Lawrence arrived at Carchemish in spring 1911. With Hogarth distantly supervising the work from Britain, Lawrence and his colleague Leonard Woolley were largely left to their own devices in running the dig.

The archeological site consisted of three huge mounds and a nearby local village whose primary source of employment came from working for the British on the dig. It was here that Lawrence's soon-to-be legendary talent for working with Arabs was first displayed. During the four archeological seasons preceding World War I, from 1911 to 1914, he ran the day-to-day operations at Carchemish brilliantly, by all accounts instilling a sense of fun into what otherwise would have been backbreaking drudgery.

Lawrence introduced a reward system for grading the quality of the finds. The overseer would fire pistol shots into the air, with the number corresponding to the object's importance; the more shots, the greater the find. The worker would then be rewarded with *baksheesh* (a small amount of money), but it was the honor of the number of shots awarded that often provoked heated arguments. Lawrence was discovering the curious mix, to Western eyes, of a culture that was partly centered on honor, partly mercenary.

Lawrence also instituted a series of races, pitting the pick men against the shovelers and the basket men, until the entire workforce was soon yelling and running at top speed. By turning the toil into a game, a day's scheduled work would often be finished by noon or earlier. While Lawrence proved to be not much of a formal scholar (during these years he published as little as he could), his genius in directing what we would today call fieldwork was perhaps the most valuable lesson he ever learned.

Leonard Woolley, who was later knighted as a tribute to his distinguished archeological career, was a kind, able, energetic, sensitive companion, who shared a house on the site with Lawrence throughout much of his time at Carchemish. Woolley was the rare man who thought

Lawrence neither cad nor god. Although he found Lawrence both charming and talented, he did not see the budding genius that so many of his supporters later perceived. With a fine eye he described the eccentric junior archeologist at this happiest time of his life. "He always wore a blazer of French grey trimmed with pink, white shorts, held up by a gaudy Arab belt with swinging tassels . . . grey stockings [socks], red Arab slippers and no hat; his hair was always very long and in wild disorder."[3] Even before he was famous, Lawrence was not likely to be overlooked.

If Lawrence found his calling at Carchemish, he also encountered the great love of his life. Dahoum (meaning "the dark one") was a servant working at the camp. Ten years Lawrence's junior, startlingly handsome, steadfastly loyal, and in awe of his new mentor, the boy became his closest companion. Lawrence went so far as to make a carving of him, naked, in sandstone, which he placed on the roof of the house he shared with Woolley. In July 1913, when Lawrence was obliged to return to England on business relating to the dig, Dahoum was one of two companions Lawrence took home with him to Oxford. There has been endless speculation about the nature of the relationship between the two; suffice it to say that, platonic or not, Lawrence never loved anyone else as much.

The initials of Dahoum's nickname, "Salim Ahmad," correspond to the mysterious S. A. to whom Lawrence would later dedicate his book, *Seven Pillars of Wisdom*. In the exquisite, soaring, and heartfelt poem opening the epic, Lawrence says of S. A. "I loved you, so I drew these tides of men into my hands and wrote my will across the sky in stars / To earn you Freedom, the seven pillared worthy house, that your eyes might be shining for me / When we came."[4] Years after Carchemish, Lawrence would write of S. A., "I wrought for him freedom to lighten his sad eyes: but he died waiting for me. So I threw my gift away and now not anywhere will I find rest and peace."[5]

Carchemish is also where the young Lawrence first met a remarkable woman. At the time of their meeting, Gertrude Bell was already a legend. She had visited portions of Arabia not seen by any westerner, let alone a woman of the cosseted Edwardian era. Even Lawrence, for all his local knowledge, admitted that there was no one in the world who so understood the differences in tribal structure in the Middle East as did Bell.

On one of her many journeys through the region, Bell came to visit Carchemish. Lawrence and Woolley, after being subjected to one of the formidable lady's lectures about their lack of archeological precision, defended themselves hotly. Lawrence, employing his charm, tuned her quite entirely around; by the time she was leaving, Bell was a stout supporter of their efforts. It would not be the last time Lawrence swayed the mercurial Bell into becoming an ally.

The visit ended on a comic note. The villagers, on learning that a lady had come to visit Lawrence and knowing him to be a bachelor, assumed a marriage was about to take place; they began planning elaborate celebrations. When Gertrude Bell left in the evening of the same day she had arrived, the locals felt outraged that Lawrence had been so rudely rejected, and he was hard-pressed to restore order. Lawrence had won over the workers to the point that they identified with him in a way entirely uncommon for the era. This initial acceptance opened the door to the local understanding that would be so central to Lawrence's emerging philosophy of nation building.

One of the reasons for this bond was that at Carchemish Lawrence treated the Arab and Kurdish workers as equals—human beings who were to be worked with, not talked down to. This was a rare attitude among Europeans of his time and social class. At Carchemish, Lawrence developed an understanding of Arab tribes and the long-standing feuds between them, their aspirations and their religion; in short he became conversant in their culture as only one who lives among another people can come to be.

This encyclopedic local knowledge of the people he was working with earned Lawrence their respect, trust, and confidence. It is not too much to say that there never would have been a Lawrence of Arabia without Carchemish and its lessons.

But Lawrence's insights during the Carchemish years were not merely cultural and philosophical. He made his first visit to a city whose name would soon be forever linked to his—Aqaba.

At the end of December 1913, Sir Frederick Kenyon of the British Museum instructed Woolley and Lawrence to join an archeological survey of Northern Sinai. Behind the academic façade, the real purpose of the expedition was to gather information about the region for British intelligence in London. Geographically, Sinai stood abreast of the British Empire's "jugular vein"—the Suez Canal, the key commercial and military passageway that linked London and India, the jewel in the crown of the empire. London considered it necessary to learn as much as possible about what had up to now seemed to be merely an obscure Ottoman Empire backwater.

While undertaking the mission, Lawrence came to Aqaba, where he noted two critical facts. All the guns in the Red Sea port pointed out to sea, and could not be turned around; the city was entirely undefended from the landward side. Second, Lawrence noted the undoubted key to the position—*Wadi Ithm,* a giant slab of rock northeast of the port, so narrow it could only be traversed by camels moving in single file; it towered over the city. To possess the Wadi Ithm was to control Aqaba. These two seemingly unimportant facts became the key to one of the most astonishing adventures in history.

In June 1914 the digging season ended as the clouds of World War I gathered. Lawrence left Carchemish, never to return or to see Dahoum again. Dahoum would die just two years later, in 1916, a victim of the famine and epidemics then sweeping his village. Of his time at Carchemish, Lawrence later wrote, "till the war swallowed up everything, I wanted nothing better than Carchemish, which was a perfect life."[6] However, as was true for many idylls predating the Great War, Carchemish was a paradise lost. After the war, Lawrence never showed any inclination to return to archeological work nor to revisit the scene of his earlier happiness. Both would prove casualties of the looming conflict, along with millions of other shattered dreams.

World War I broke out in August 1914. With Hogarth's help, Lawrence received a temporary appointment as Second Lieutenant in the British Army. He joined the geographical survey of the army's general staff, where his knowledge of the Middle East could be put to good use in map-making. He followed his department to Cairo in December 1914, where he was made part of the intelligence section. Between 1914 and 1916, Lawrence put together large-scale maps of Sinai, wrote geographical digests, tracked the movements of Turkish forces, and interrogated prisoners.

To the casual observer at the time, Lawrence did not appear to have the makings of much of a soldier. His hair remained long, as he had worn it in Carchemish. He casually sauntered across rooms; he did not march. He ignored salutes with the same frequency that he refused to give them. He uniform was permanently disheveled, with unpressed trousers, unpolished buttons, his belt dangling. He wore patent-leather evening shoes rather than boots and a blood-red tie rather than the standard-issue khaki.

Lawrence, like many other Middle Eastern scholars including Bell, Woolley, and his erstwhile boss Hogarth, were to form the nucleus of what would be the intelligence gathering department for British forces in the Middle East. Active in advocating and pursuing policies on the ground, they came to be far more than spies or mere analysts; they became implementers of British imperial policy, "doers" as well as "thinkers." This dual role suited Lawrence perfectly.

Lieutenant Colonel Gilbert "Bertie" Clayton, one of the most powerful British officers in Egypt during the war, directed all the intelligence services in Cairo. He was a permanent official, whose local knowledge and bureaucratic savvy made him more powerful than many of the transitory generals and civilian officials he supposedly was there to serve; he ended the war a general. Shrewd, sober, quiet, sensible, and steady, Clayton was a veteran of the British-dominated Egyptian army, and was a confidant of the greatest British imperialist of the age, Lord Kitchener.

In fact, Clayton had fought alongside Field Marshall Kitchener at his most famous battle, Omdurman, in September 1898, where the British took revenge for the murder of Gordon of Khartoum, and secured their African Empire. Having carte blanche to run all intelligence operations in the Egyptian theater, Clayton was well respected by his subordinates, as he tended to give them a great deal of leeway. He was to become an influential patron to Lawrence.

The intelligence department also included two members of parliament (MPs) who had specialized knowledge of the region, George Lloyd and Aubrey Herbert. Herbert, the younger son of the Earl of Caernarvon and a product of Eton, knew the Ottoman capital, Constantinople, well. An aristocrat to his fingertips, he oozed self-assurance. He was later immortalized as the character Sandy Arbuthnot in John Buchan's great World War I thriller, *Greenmantle.* Herbert and Lawrence were always half-attracted, half-repelled by each other. Lawrence, while warming to Herbert, suggested that he was "a joke, but a very nice one."[7] Herbert, in turn, saw Lawrence as "half cad," but admitted that he had a touch of genius.

Herbert, like Lawrence and most of the rest of those working in Cairo intelligence, was pushing for a British invasion of the Ottoman Empire, Berlin's ally in the Great War. While Germany was undoubtedly Britain's primary enemy in the conflict, in the Middle East it was the collision of the British and this Turkish-dominated empire that was the primary strategic clash, as their lands sat uneasily adjacent to one another.

Lawrence's comfortable life in Cairo, where he lounged at the opulent Grand Continental Hotel while millions of Allied soldiers were dying on the Western Front in the stalemated battle in the trenches with the Kaiser's Germany, increasingly made him feel guilty. The tragic losses of men on the front lines came to include two of Lawrence's brothers. In May 1915, Frank was killed by shellfire, and Will was shot down in October of that year, while serving in the Royal Flying Corps. Lawrence chafed all the more at his secure existence.

Finally, in spring 1916, Lawrence and Herbert were sent on a daring mission. They were ordered to proceed to the town of Kut-al-Mahra in Mesopotamia (today's Iraq), in order to bribe the Turkish commander there, Khalit Pasha, into allowing the surrounded Sixth Division of the Indian army, led by General Sir Charles Townshend, to escape. In trying to conquer Mesopotamia, which would have been a crippling blow to the Ottoman Empire, Townshend had already suffered 10,000 casualties. His troops bogged down in the heat, strayed far from their secure supply lines in the Persian Gulf, and ran into determined Turkish resistance. Finally, their flanks turned, they were entirely surrounded by Ottoman forces. Another 23,000 casualties resulted from failed British efforts to rescue Townshend's Sixth Indian division. Thirteen thousand five hundred of his men remained cut off. Herbert and Lawrence were authorized to offer Khalit Pasha up to two million pounds to let them go.

Unfortunately for the British, Khalit was already wealthy. He was also the nephew of Enver Pasha, first among equals in the Ottoman Empire's wartime government. It is a telling sign of the unreality surrounding this first invasion of Mesopotamia that anyone seriously thought there was a chance that Khalit would betray his family and his country.

The tragedy at Kut was the second great blow to Britain's efforts to defeat Turkey, ranking with the fighting at Gallipoli, Britain's earlier doomed effort to capture Constantinople, as a disaster for British arms. Of the 13,500 men who surrendered to Khalit, over 4,000 died during an epic march from Kut to prison camps in Turkey. General Townshend, however, was treated with respect by the Ottomans and billeted in an opulent hotel on the Bosporus, never once inquiring about the fate of his men for the rest of the war. Nothing that happened during this sorry episode did anything to dissuade Lawrence from his view that regular army officers were criminally letting down his country.

Upon his return to Cairo from the failed Kut mission, Lawrence learned of the founding of a new British intelligence service, the Arab Bureau. His old mentor Hogarth, now a lieutenant commander in the Royal Navy, had been authorized by Clayton in 1916 to set up the new service, which was bureaucratically answerable not to the military but to a civilian authority, in this case jointly the British Foreign Office and the War Department.

Headquartered in Cairo's Savoy Hotel, the Arab Bureau was responsible for assessing political developments in the Middle East and came to manage the formulation and implementation of British policy. Lawrence, while initially refused entry into the bureau, was nonetheless given the task of editing its influential summary, the *Arab Bulletin*.

Frustrated at finding himself once again behind a desk and being denied a reunion with Hogarth, Lawrence proceeded to make himself insufferable, plaguing the senior officers who had casually rejected his transfer. Lawrence would return their reports to them for correction, with their grammatical mistakes circled in red pen. Finally, after such behavior took its toll, Lawrence was allowed to undertake a second mission in the field, this time accompanying Ronald Storrs of the Arab Bureau to western Arabia, to get a sense of the possibilities for success of the then fading Arab Revolt against the Turks. After years of frustration in Cairo, from this moment on Lawrence never looked back.

The story of the Arab Revolt begins with an assassination. In 1880, the uncle of the man who was to become king of the Hejaz (western

Arabia) was viciously stabbed to death on the streets of Jeddah, the port city of Mecca. He had been conspiring against his Turkish overlords with his nephew, the future King Hussein, who never forgave the Ottomans for killing his beloved mentor.

By the early twentieth century, the Ottoman Empire's control of their Arab territories was precarious. Arabs made up almost half the Empire's population of 22 million subjects; the 10.5 million Arabs dwarfed the numbers of their Turkish overlords, who accounted for only 7.5 million people. Further, five-sixths of the Hejazis lived as nomads or semi-nomads. Thus, even before the war, the Turks controlled Hejazi cities while the *Bedu* (Arab bedouin) de facto ruled the rest of the country.

The geography of the Hejaz made it almost impossible to control. Large sections of it were arid desert, empty of both man and beast. About 750 miles long and, at its widest, almost 200 miles across, the Hejaz managed to support a population estimated at 300,000. Although it had long formed a part of the Ottoman Empire, its distance from Constantinople, coupled with the region's primitive state of transport and communications, had always given it a great deal of autonomy.

The staple crop of western Arabia was dates; but the real money-maker was controlling the *haj,* the annual pilgrimage of the 70,000 followers of Islam who journeyed to Mecca each year, as they are required to at least once in their lives by the Koran, the Muslim holy book. The central government in Constantinople in effect paid extortion money to the Bedu not to prey overmuch on the *haj* pilgrims. This cash flow, in addition to providing guides for the Muslim travelers from abroad, sustained the Hejazi economy.

The Hashemite family to which both Hussein and his uncle belonged was the most respected in the Islamic world; they could trace their descent back 37 generations to the Prophet Mohammed himself, through his daughter Fatima. Following his uncle's death, Hussein continued to plot and scheme against the Turks, so in 1893 the Ottomans exiled him to their capital city, Constantinople, so as to keep a better eye on him.

Somewhat surprisingly, given the cutthroat world of Ottoman politics, Hussein was not murdered. For the next 16 years he lived under glorified house arrest, using much of his time to meditate but never losing the desire to return to the Hejaz as emir. A small, hard man, with a bushy beard, delicate hands, and fine features, Hussein was opinionated, domineering, yet polite, possessing the courtly manners of an earlier age. He was well educated, knowing much of religion, classical Arab poetry, and nature, but behind this sophisticated façade, his drive for power and intrigue was almost limitless.

In 1908, the Young Turk rebellion, a last-ditch effort by a group of army officers inspired by Western ideals to modernize the decaying Ottoman Empire, took power away from the Ottoman sultan. The revolutionaries' political arm, the Committee of Union and Progress (CUP), dismissed the ruling Hejazi emir (a distant relative of Hussein's) for corruption. Ironically, it was at the sultan's insistence that the CUP was forced, against its better judgment, to end Hussein's exile and place him on the throne of the Hejaz. In his favor were all those years of living quietly in Constantinople, his family's unimpeachable lineage, and his obvious erudition. But the CUP had been right to be nervous, because, from the beginning, Hussein set out to carve as much autonomy for himself as possible; he had no intention of merely serving as a vassal of far-away Constantinople.

In line with their overall centralizing mission, the CUP pushed forward with plans to extend the Hejaz railway, which ran between Damascus and Medina, Islam's second holiest city. The Young Turks wanted to extend the line to Mecca and Jeddah, farther down the Red Sea coast.

This plan posed a serious threat to both the Hashemites and the Bedu. As Hussein made clear to a gathering of Bedu chieftains, "The railway will ruin you completely . . . Once the Turks can rush troops from one part of the Hejaz to the other, they will no longer need to pay gold to the Bedu."[8] Increasingly, the Hashemites and the Bedu shared core interests against Constantinople, which was aiming to curtail both the economic and political independence of the area.

The Bedu stood to lose their lucrative control of the pilgrim routes to the holy cities of Mecca and Medina. The expansion of the railway and the coming of the telegraph to the Hejaz would also allow the CUP to exercise, for the first time, direct control over the emir. If the plan was carried out, Hussein at best would become merely a regional placeholder for the Ottomans, rather than the semi-independent ruler he was used to being.

As war broke out in 1914, the Ottoman Empire joined Germany and Austria-Hungary against Britain, France, and Russia. Hussein, predictably, played a double game, trying to keep his political options open. Early in the war, Hussein's second and favorite son, Abdullah, was sought out by British intelligence who wanted to know where his father's loyalties lay. Abdullah replied that the Hashemites would remain neutral at present, but indicated that with sufficient British support (and presumably a significant territorial reward) they could be induced to revolt against the Turks.

And, indeed, Hussein proved so lukewarm a supporter of the Ottoman Empire that he infuriated the CUP. Early in the war the Young Turks played the jihad card, calling on their Muslim co-religionists throughout the world to rise up and fight the hated Christian powers. They counted on the Hashemites, as direct descendents of the Prophet, to play a major role in the jihad campaign.

This policy confirmed the worst fears of British imperialists, to whom the vision of millions of Muslims revolting in British India was apocalyptic. However, the diplomatic maneuver came to nothing. Hussein failed to endorse the call, blandly explaining to the CUP that since the Hejaz was dependent on grain imports from India, any British embargo that would likely result from such Hashemite support for Constantinople's jihad, could leave the region devastated by famine. The CUP, angered beyond measure, began to plot the removal of Hussein, through assassination if necessary.

The Ottoman's hard-line governor, their man on the ground in the Hejaz, Vehib Pasha, was the principal force behind efforts to depose or kill the obstinate emir. He lost (or, more likely, had stolen from him) a trunk containing compromising documents about the scheme, which wound up in the hands of Ali, Hussein's eldest son. By early 1915, the emir had concrete proof of Constantinople's treachery. Wanting to avoid his uncle's fate, Hussein began, in turn, to scheme. His desire for both physical and political survival threw him into the waiting arms of the British.

Hussein sent his third son, Feisal, to Damascus to explore the possibility of an alliance with the secret societies then honeycombing Syrian politics, who shared the goal of independence from Constantinople. One of the most prominent, al-Fatat, called on the emir to lead an Arab revolt against continued Turkish rule, pledging loyalty to him. Later, this would prove a key argument for Lawrence as to why the Hashemites enjoyed genuine political legitimacy in Greater Syria; local Syrian leaders had invited Hussein and his sons to take charge of their war for liberation.

When an Arab intelligence source, claiming to represent al-Ahd, another of the major Syrian secret societies, confirmed to the British that Hussein, the sherif (a descendent of Mohammed, a nobleman) of Mecca spoke for more than just the Hejazis, both Clayton and Lawrence, who were following these developments from Cairo, were beside themselves with delight. An organic effort at subversion of the Ottomans seemed to be brewing. On August 18, 1915, Hussein sent a letter to the British High Commissioner in Cairo, Sir Hugh MacMahon, asking what political inducements the British might offer him in return for rising up against the Turks. Almost daily, the plotting was growing more serious and concrete.

The effectiveness of the Turkish espionage service forced Hussein's hand. By the fall of 1915, the Ottomans had begun to roll back their enemies in Syria, rounding up the secret societies the Hashemites had been plotting with. Hussein could not be certain that, under torture, the members of al-Ahd and al-Fatat would not betray him, revealing that he was openly negotiating with the British.

Then, in April 1916, Djemal Pasha, a member of the CUP ruling triumvirate and in overall charge of the region, told Hussein that 3,500 specially trained Ottoman troops would be marching through the Hejaz on their way to the tip of the Arabian Peninsula, where they would be building a telegraph station. Both the march and the telegraph were direct threats to the emir. Hussein knew that Djemal Pasha's troops could

easily crush the Hashemites as they marched through, while the telegraph would make Ottoman efforts to quickly respond to any future revolt far more effective. By the spring of 1916, it was clear to Hussein
that he had little choice but to rise up. The Arab Revolt began in June
1916, when Hussein fired the symbolic first shot of the campaign from
his balcony in Mecca.

The British did not have a better alternative to bankrolling
Hashemite subversion in order to defeat the Turks. In the first part of
1916, they were still smarting from their earlier failures at Gallipoli and
Kut while also gearing up for an expected third Turkish assault on the
Suez Canal. They had run out of options for dealing with the eastern
theater of the war. At the time, they needed Hussein as much as he
needed them.

Still, the actual timing of the start of the Arab Revolt surprised the
British High Command. With the Turkish authorities closing in, Hussein had little choice but to rise up. It was then or never. But Hussein
had not been able to nail down either British territorial inducements
or concrete offers of assistance before time ran out. This was to prove
a fatal mistake for the Hashemites, as it forced them to rely on future
British goodwill.

Events had moved in the direction Lawrence's colleagues were
hoping for. Almost since the war began, even before Lawrence had
been allowed to join the intelligence service, the Arab Bureau had
urged that the British support an Arab uprising against their far-away
Turkish overlords. Attacking the Turks through their restive subject
peoples in the Middle East made perfect sense to the scholar/spies in
the bureau, who had such an intimate understanding of the tensions
in the region. That fall, Lawrence was sent to Arabia, to get a feel for

which of Hussein's many sons was the best candidate for British aid. It was there, at Hamra, that Lawrence met Prince Feisal.

Lawrence's trip to Arabia was the seemingly most unromantic of missions: to make a cost-benefit analysis of the viability of the Arab Revolt, and to see if he could find a leader to keep it afloat. Since Emir Hussein had launched the rebellion, in June 1916, Arab fortunes had turned ever blacker. The worst came with a frontal assault on Medina. The Arab Bedu fighters, unaccustomed to modern weapons such as artillery and airplanes, had been butchered before its gates; those who weren't killed or wounded fled, leaving Medina securely in Turkish hands. Before the British invested more supplies and money in the Arab Revolt, they needed assurances that that such an expenditure would not be made in vain.

It had not been easy for Lawrence to get himself assigned to the mission. He had previously sought permission to travel inland in Arabia to meet with Emir Hussein, which had been refused. It was only when Ronald Storrs, the oriental secretary (chief political officer) to the British High Commissioner, was directed to travel to Arabia, that Lawrence got his chance. Storrs was just the sort of man Lawrence was able to impress—a lover of art and music, vain, suave, and sophisticated. Storrs fought through the British red tape in Cairo, having Lawrence temporarily seconded to the Arab Bureau at last. Lawrence was thus permitted to accompany Storrs to Arabia. Once again, he had secured a vital mentor to plead his case with the world.

The British were determined to hedge their bets in the Hejaz. Part of Storrs's mission was to relay to Prince Abdullah the unhappy news that the British would not supply the Arab Revolt with British troops, that 10,000 pounds that had been promised them was not going to be paid, and that air support was being withdrawn from the Red Sea port of Rabegh. While it would be useful to the British if the revolt were to flower, with the carnage in the trenches along the Western Front, war in Arabia was a luxury that would be quickly dispensed with if it appeared that the hopes of success were bleak.

It was into this do-or-die situation that Storrs and Lawrence arrived in Jeddah in Arabia, October 19, 1916. Lawrence was to monitor the situation, assess if the revolt was viable, find a leader from among Hussein's many sons, then report back to Cairo. He had been invited to Arabia as an afterthought.

Storrs and Lawrence first met with Abdullah, the sherif's political confidant. Lawrence, while respectful of Hussein's favorite son, came away disliking him, as he saw him as clever but lazy. While he believed that Abdullah was intelligent and popular, Lawrence felt he lacked the drive to lead the Arab Revolt. Abdullah later came to dislike Lawrence as well, feeling that he received too much credit for what were really his family's subsequent accomplishments. He also resented the fact that Lawrence favored his younger brother. However, at the time, he agreed with Storrs (who also received Hussein's critical, if grumpy, acquiescence over the phone,) that Lawrence should travel inland to seek out Feisal.

Upon meeting Feisal at Hamra in the fertile region of *Wadi Safra*, with its mud-brick houses and gentle palm trees, Hussein's shrewdest son asked Lawrence what he thought of the place. Lawrence's legendary response was that he liked it well, but it is far from Damascus.[9] In saying this, Lawrence shook Feisal to his core. Lawrence had given voice to what Feisal was thinking, to what was in his imagination. Lawrence's love of medieval derring-do, the focus of his study at Oxford as well as of his youthful dreams, melded perfectly with the Arabs' romantic notions about their own glorious past. With this remark, he had turned the Hashemite revolt into a crusade to retake Damascus, the scene of so much past Arab glory, and transformed the revolt into an exercise in Arab self-regeneration. This idealistic sense of a war to redeem past glories would continue to infuse the Arab Revolt until the capture of Damascus, which became its glorious all-consuming goal, and saw Feisal's army through many perilous times. Despite Lawrence's role, this was to be primarily an Arab enterprise. As Lawrence later wrote, "I had preached to Feisal, from our first meeting, that freedom was taken, not given."[10]

More practically, Lawrence came to believe that Feisal's 4,000 men, if properly led, adequately armed, and, most importantly, allowed to fight as they always had done, could defeat the mighty Turkish Empire. But it must be a guerrilla, rather than a conventional campaign. The Arabs used the desert as a ship uses the sea; to turn them into third-rate conventional troops, as the British had done up to then, was to doom the Arab cause to defeat. Rather, Lawrence hoped to build on this Arab advantage; they would use the desert as they always had, hitting the enemy and stealthily retreating again, moving far more quickly over the forbidding terrain, while the impotent Turks would cower behind city walls.

Having begun to convince Feisal to adopt this fundamental change in military strategy, Lawrence hurried back to Cairo, where he was persuasive enough to convince the British High Command to send him back to Feisal as an advisor, a post he retained from November 1916 until October 1918. But the job description "advisor" does not begin to convey what Lawrence was to the revolt. He was the senior military and political confidant to Feisal, a commander of Arab guerilla units, and, from July 1917 on, in charge of coordinating Anglo-Arab military planning.

Lawrence was predominant in organizing, coordinating, and shaping the immediate goals of the Arab Revolt. Conceiving, as no one had, the possibilities the struggle allowed for Arab self-regeneration, he was able to obtain vital British support for the enterprise. More than this, he became its chief strategist and ideologist, creating an effective guerrilla movement of national liberation.[11] From that first meeting with Feisal, Lawrence imbued the Arab Revolt with meaning, making it a cause worth fighting and dying for.

Chapter 2

"We are calling them to fight for us on a lie, and I can't stand it."

—Lawrence in a note to Glibert Clayton, May 1917

Lawrence's contemporaneous account of Feisal is telling. Written in November 1916, Lawrence describes the emir as, "tall, graceful, almost regal in appearance. Aged thirty-one. Very quick and restless in movement. Far more imposing personally than any of his brothers, he knows it and trades on it. Is as clear-skinned as a pure Circassian, with dark hair, vivid black eyes set a little sloping in his face, strong nose, short chin. Looks like a European, and very like the monument of Richard I at Fontevraud."[1] If Lawrence saw the desert war as a crusade, Feisal was his Richard the Lionheart.

By December 1916, the revolt's fortunes had begun to turn for the better. The Turks had tried and failed to conquer the strategic Arabian port of Yenbo. The following month, moving up the western side of the

Arabian Peninsula, British and Arab forces captured Wejh, another key port city. But both of these triumphs were largely the work of the British navy and its sailors, with the Arabs playing a secondary role. As winter gave way to spring, Lawrence hit upon an audacious plan that would place the Arabs firmly in the starring role in the war for their national liberation.

With Feisal's trust in him growing, Lawrence worked to persuade the cautious prince that a strike on the vital port of Aqaba to the north was the key to Arabia and would transform the rebellion. From Aqaba, the Royal Navy could quickly resupply Feisal from the Red Sea, as the city was geographically much closer to both Cairo and Damascus. Control of Aqaba would seal Feisal's victory in Arabia and prove crucial for the coming Syrian campaign.

Having visited Aqaba just before the war, Lawrence had local knowledge that the defenses surrounding the port pointed out to sea; that the city was vulnerable to an attack from the landward desert side. The Turks had not bothered to build up these defenses since no one thought it possible that the scorching desert around the city could be crossed; any attackers attempting to traverse the inferno would have to depend on a paltry number of wells, and water would not be sufficient to supply a large number of troops. Lawrence, starting with a ridiculously small force of 36 men, hoped to recruit Bedu as he went, relying on local sympathy. This was the way around the supposedly impregnable desert.

Only one man could make Lawrence's plan a reality—Auda Abu Tayyi, the larger-than-life chief of the Howeitat, whom Lawrence first met at Wejh in April 1917. Lawrence's circular route through the desert would pass through the territories of the Ageyl, Ateiba, Billie, Harb,

and Juheima tribes, but Auda and his people controlled much of northern Arabia. The Howeitat would have to supply the active local political support for the plan, in terms of volunteering as Lawrence's small
force moved north, if the assault was to come off. Lawrence beguiled the
Howeitat chief with his charm, the sheer audacity of the undertaking,
and dreams of glory and especially plunder, and offered him 10,000
pounds sterling. All were essential to persuade him, that and Lawrence's
promise that there were sufficient funds to recruit Bedu as the party
progressed.

If Lawrence's epic was to have Feisal as a modern King Arthur,
surely in his own inimitable way Auda was to serve the role as one of the
knights-errant of the enterprise. A story Lawrence told about Auda
shortly after the war is illustrative of the timeless uniqueness of the
Howeitat leader:

> Auda came to Wejh and swore allegiance to the Sherif in the pictur-
> esque Arab formula, on the book [the Koran], and then sat down to
> dinner with Feisal. Halfway through the meal he rose with an apol-
> ogy, and withdrew from the tent. We heard the noise of hammering
> without, and saw Auda beating something between two great stones.
> When he came back he craved pardon of the Sherif for having inad-
> vertently eaten his bread with Turkish teeth, and displayed the bro-
> ken remains of his rather fine Damascus set in his hand.
> Unfortunately, he could hardly eat anything at all afterwards, and
> went very sorrowfully till in Aqaba the British High Commissioner
> sent him an Egyptian dentist who refurbished his mouth.[2]

This was certainly not an ordinary man.

The most feared warrior in Arabia, Auda was tall, wiry, powerful,
with the hooked nose of a predatory bird and brown-green eyes. In his
thirties at the time of the revolt, he was still as active as a much younger

man. He had been married 28 times and wounded 13. It was said that Auda had personally killed 75 men in hand-to-hand fighting since 1900, excluding Turks, whom he did not think worth counting. He was reputed to have torn out and eaten the hearts of several of his many enemies. While on campaign, he would sing to himself or recount epic stories of his old raids. Ostentatious in his manner of cultivating both friends and enemies, Auda would impulsively and scandalously insult others to their faces for no apparent reason, defying them to challenge him to battle. At the same time, his lavish hospitality was legendary throughout the Arabian Peninsula.

Fortunately for Lawrence, Auda had a grudge against the Ottomans. In 1909 he had killed a Turkish policeman who had unwisely demanded tax money of him, and had since then been on the run from the government. He was eager to punish the Turks for their impudence. His authority over his followers and others in Feisal's camp was due to his courage, his dash, and his energy. Lawrence wryly observed that Auda was "warmly loved even by those to whom he is most trying—his friends."[3]

The Abu Tayyi branch of the Howeitat tribe was acclaimed as the most effective raiders in Arabia. Numbering only about 500 fighters, they were unruly, anarchic individualists, like their leader. They were to be the primary material through which Lawrence was to work his miracle.

The Aqaba campaign reads like one of the feudal romances Lawrence so dearly loved. On May 9, 1917, setting off from Wejh, Lawrence disappeared into the desert. Sherif Nasir, whom Lawrence considered one of the ablest guerilla fighters in the Hashemite army, accompanied him as Feisal's chief representative. Nasir had taken charge of 25,000 pounds in gold (the Bedu did not value paper notes) that would be needed to pay volunteers along the way. Auda was also with him, along with his nephew, the notorious raider, Zaal, and only 34 others. Lawrence and Auda had talked Feisal into granting them leave to attempt the impossible. As for the British, Lawrence was on his own; the Aqaba operation had not been authorized by any senior British commander. Indeed, his superiors in Cairo were only dimly aware of his movements in the Hejaz at the best of times.

So as not to alert the Turks, Lawrence and Auda planned a circular route to Aqaba, 800 miles in length. It was May, already high summer in Arabia. The heat shimmered off the rocks in waves, and the sun suffocated efforts at breathing. As often happened in the moments of crisis in his life, Lawrence's fever and boils returned, first contracted while on his Oxford undergraduate journey. He was heading into country where few westerners had ever been before, with the exception of his redoubtable friend, Gertrude Bell.

The small party started out across the Nefudh desert, a place so inhospitable that soon there were literally no tracks in the sand to indicate the presence of any other form of life. While crossing the Nefudh the party ran headlong into the teeth of a whirling sandstorm, complete with dust devils that could well have been the pillars of fire described in the Bible. The raiders rejoiced when they at last came upon ostrich tracks, as it meant the worst of the crossing was over. The desert, playing its eternally contradictory role, was an enemy far more formidable than the Turks, as well as the Arab's golden means of victory.

Along the march, one of the men, Gasim, became disoriented and fell behind, Lawrence decided to go back for him, risking both his own life and the daring objective of the Aqaba raid. Riding directly into the sun, with only his army compass to guide him, Lawrence found Gasim wandering deliriously in the blazing Arabian sun; miraculously, the two men made it back to the main party. An unimpressed Auda said only that Gasim's life was not worth the price of a camel. But the tribesmen, already in awe of him, began to view Lawrence as a superior being. Gasim's rescue became part of the Lawrence mythology, setting him as a man apart.

On May 30, 1917, Howeitat warriors under Ali Abu Fitna joined the small raiding party, while Auda went barnstorming across the countryside, going on to meet Nuri Shalaan, the paramount chief of the Rwalla tribe, hoping to enlist his aid. While Bedu recruits gathered by Auda reconnoitered east of Maan, near Aqaba, Lawrence went on a solitary reconnaissance mission around Damascus, far to the north. Ostensibly, he was going there to make contact with Syrian Bedu tribes for possible recruitment. In reality the trip, which would take him 560 miles through enemy-held territory, more accurately resembled a death wish. Before heading north, he left a note for his superior, Clayton, in Cairo, saying, "Clayton, I've decided to go off alone to Damascus, hoping to get myself killed on the way: for all sakes try and clear this show up before it goes further. We are calling them to fight for us on a lie, and I can't stand it."[4]

The Arab Bedu were becoming increasingly suspicious of vague and contradictory British promises. When Nuri Shalaan first met Lawrence, he demanded to know which British promises to believe. Rumors of a treaty between Britain and France that carved much of the Middle East between them to the exclusion of the Arabs had just begun to surface. Out in the field, Lawrence found himself on the receiving end of Arab anger and suspicion, and, with Auda gone, he had begun to crack under the strain. Lawrence, despite his efforts, survived his reconnaissance and returned to the main Arab camp. Meanwhile, Auda had done his work well. He had recruited 535 Howeitat, 150 Rwalla and Shararat, and 35 Kawakiba Bedu. On June 20, 1917, leaving 200 men behind to guard the tents at Wadi Sirhan, over 500 battle-hardened men, with Lawrence and Auda in the lead, headed out into the desert again.

While not guessing their ultimate goal, the Turks caught wind that there was an Arab force in the area. From now on, as they crossed the desert, Lawrence's raiders came across destroyed wells—the Turks hoped to let the desert and logistics take care of their enemies. However, the Turks proved inept at limiting the water supply. On the way to the outskirts of Aqaba, the Arabs came across three wells that had been mangled; however, two had been only slightly damaged and were salvageable.

A great problem for Lawrence was the shortage of funds to pay the Bedu. Nasir had run through the British money on Auda's mission to recruit the tribes and was now forced to pay newcomers in promissory notes, which the Bedu thought worthless. Finally, with funds running low and Arab endurance stretched to even its formidable limits, the raiders caught a break. On June 30, at El-Jefer, Auda's own permanent headquarters, just as the lack of water was catching up to the raiding party at last, they came across another well, Auda's own property, which still functioned. Digging it out, the Arabs, with a serviceable well, now had a chance to take nearby Aqaba, their glittering prize.

The climactic battle for Aqaba took place just outside the city, at the oasis Aba l-Lissan, on July 2, 1917. The Arabs took the Turks by complete surprise. Better still, they fell upon them sleeping in a natural depression around the spring there; Lawrence's raiders had the great advantage of claiming the high ground. Their snipers encircled the Turkish camp. Auda's nephew Zaal and Bedu horsemen cut the telegraph wires to Maan, ensuring that there would be no Turkish reinforcements. It was an especially scalding day. Lawrence later remembered that the battle took place in "a heat that made movement torture. The burning ground seared the forearms of our snipers."[5] Things were not any better for the Turks. Blinded by the sun and confused by the shadows from the overhanging rock where the Arabs had ensconced themselves, their return fire was entirely ineffective.

At this critical juncture, with neither side effectively striking the other, Lawrence used a ploy that reflected the knowledge of local tribal culture he had gained by working with the Arabs in the archeological digs years before. In what was to be the pivotal moment of both the campaign and his life, he crept to a cleft in the rocks of Aba l-Lissan searching for a precious gulp of water. Nasir joined him there, then Auda. Lawrence, in anger, laid down the gauntlet to warriors steeped in their own honor culture. Acidly observing that the Howeitat seemed to shoot a great deal, but managed to hit nothing, he waited for the response.

Stalking off in a fury, Auda placed himself at the vanguard of around 50 Howeitat and charged straight into the befuddled Turkish lines. Though his horse fell, Auda's charge broke the enemy, who scrambled away in utter confusion. Lawrence, riding behind, later discovered that in the chaos and excitement, he had shot his own camel in the back of the head. But, miraculously, the assault had succeeded. At Aba l-Lissan an entire Turkish battalion was wiped out, either killed or forced to surrender. The Arabs killed 300 Turkish soldiers and took 160 prisoners, while, astonishingly, losing only two of their own men. Wadi Ithm, commanding the high ground around an Aqaba with its guns impotently pointing out to sea, lay open to them. Lawrence and the Arabs had triumphed.

After the smashing victory at Aba l-Lissan, a further 1,000 Howeitat tribesmen swelled Arab numbers. Lawrence managed to take Aqaba itself without firing another shot. While the Turkish garrison there remained formidable, the Turks, having no real intelligence of the marauding force and fearing the worst, believed that they were heavily outnumbered. Capturing a Turkish sentry, the Arabs gave him a gold sovereign to tell his Turkish commanders that the Arabs would kill every inhabitant of the garrison unless they surrendered immediately. By midmorning the next day, the Turkish command agreed. On July 6, 1917, after an epic 800-mile journey, Lawrence and his Arab allies had come out of the desert sun, marching into Aqaba, and ended the campaign by dangling their feet in the Red Sea.

With Aqaba in the hands of the Arabs, the war in the Hejaz was effectively over. Now, the Royal Navy had the use of every major Red Sea port to resupply their Arab allies. An intelligence report written in the immediate wake of Aqaba put Turkish casualties for the campaign at 700 killed and 600 taken prisoner. Arab losses were a minuscule 4 dead and 5 wounded in actual fighting.[6] It was the most astonishing achievement of Lawrence's career, accomplished despite the longest odds, with the fewest men, and the most audacious of plans, for the highest strategic gain.

However, there was little time to reflect on the supreme accomplishment of Aqaba. The city itself had largely been destroyed by Royal Navy shelling of weeks before; as such, there was nothing left for Auda and his men to loot. Morale plummeted further as Lawrence had run out of gold and had little food, either for his now 2,000 men or their 600 Turkish prisoners. Things were so bad that the Hashemite force was reduced to eating its own transport animals to stay alive. The only way to keep the victorious troops in the field was for Lawrence to quickly make it back to Cairo, so that the British could make good on the promises he had made to his Arab comrades throughout the campaign.

An exhausted Lawrence, with 12 reliable Howeitat tribesmen in tow, crossed the Sinai desert, a 170-mile ride across near-waterless terrain, to the British High Command. His arrival at Cairo coincided with the appointment of General Sir Edmund Allenby as commander-in-chief. In early 1917, under Allenby's predecessor General Murray, British forces had twice attacked Gaza, only to be thrown back by the Turks with 6,000 casualties. Allenby, who had a sterling record as a cavalry officer in the Boer War in South Africa at the turn of the century, was one of the few British commanders to make a name for himself on the Western Front. He had been brought to Cairo to instill a needed sense of discipline and success into the ragtag forces in theater, and to provide sound strategic thinking. He was not to disappoint his superiors in London.

More importantly for Lawrence, Allenby had had enough experience fighting Boer rebels to appreciate how small numbers of guerillas could tip the strategic balance. Moreover, Allenby wholly trusted Clayton, who asserted that Lawrence alone had the confidence of Feisal and his sherifs and could maintain the Arab Revolt in the field.

Upon their first meeting, Lawrence, straight from the desert, entered Allenby's office, theatrically dressed in soiled Arab clothes and barefoot. As Lawrence wryly observed, on meeting the general and first telling him the wondrous tale of Aqaba, "Allenby could not make out how much was genuine performer and how much charlatan."[7]

What Lawrence thought of Allenby was apparent. Taking the place of Hogarth, Allenby became another father figure for him, as he came nearest, in Lawrence's words, to satisfying his "longings for a master."[8] During the war they worked together closely and amicably, under great pressure, and achieved undeniable results.

But what Allenby genuinely thought of Lawrence is far less clear. After the war, Allenby frankly stated that he thought Lawrence a brilliant war leader and that his efforts made an invaluable contribution to the ultimate British success in the Middle East. Yet he also claimed that in reality the Arabs had been no more than a minor annoyance for the Turks, and that there were other British officers who might have been even more effective than Lawrence. Suffice it to say that whatever Allenby actually thought about Lawrence, he was enough of a realist to know that anything Lawrence accomplished in the upcoming Syrian campaign would tie-up Turkish forces, to the great advantage of Allenby's regulars.

Allenby gave Lawrence many of the desperately needed supplies he wanted—200,000 pounds, 20,000 rifles, 20 Lewis machine-guns, 8 Stokes mortars, and several armored cars. What particularly impressed Allenby was that Lawrence did not ask for British troops, as that would not have suited a hard-pressed London hanging on by a thread on the Western Front in Europe. Very soon after the meeting between Allenby and Lawrence, by July 13, the British battleship HMS *Dufferin* was anchored off Aqaba, and began unloading food and arms to the Arab victors. The Aqaba victory had convinced Cairo that Lawrence was crucial to the success of the Arab Revolt, just as his delivering supplies from the British superpower convinced the Arabs that Lawrence had real sway with the British government. Lawrence had made himself indispensable to both the British and the Arabs.

Lawrence used the Aqaba victory to enhance his bureaucratic position in Cairo. Just promoted to major, he wanted and was granted a free hand in all British dealings with Feisal. He also requested that he report directly to Allenby. This very unusual request was granted, effectively placing Lawrence beyond the control of the stifling British bureaucracy he so despised. For Aqaba, Lawrence was made a Companion of the Bath. He also received the French *Croix de Guerre,* which was particularly ludicrous, since he had, controversially, already come around to the belief that the French would emerge after the war as the primary British-Arab enemy in the region. Feisal's troops were put under Allenby's direct command, forming the right wing of his army for the push on Damascus. After Aqaba, both Lawrence and his Arabs were a force that had to be taken seriously.

For all the glittering triumph Aqaba represents, it is probably Lawrence's guerilla strategy that accounts for his greatest military impact on the Arab Revolt. For the port served as the major conduit for gold and guns for Lawrence's unfolding Syrian guerrilla campaign. However, Lawrence had already conceived the best means for fighting the Turks prior to Aqaba.

Early in the revolt, Feisal's men were repulsed by the Turks in front of the gates of Medina. The defeat became a symbol of Arab impotence, and a lingering humiliation that rankled the Hashemites. As the fortunes of war began to turn in their favor, it was commonly thought that another assault must be made to take the second holiest site in Islam.

Lawrence had other ideas. On March 15, 1917, while conferring with Feisal's brother Abdullah at his camp, Lawrence once again fell ill with malaria and dysentery; being confined to bed provided a rare chance for him to think deeply and undisturbed over the next few days. It was at this point that he hatched his innovative guerrilla strategy.

However, what Lawrence propounded was not entirely novel. It bore a passing resemblance to an earlier plan concocted by Aziz Ali al-Masri, a brilliant Arab defector from the Turkish army who had played an important early role in organizing the Arab forces. Al-Masri had proposed organizing the Arab army around a series of flying columns, designed to ruin the Hejaz railway, while never fighting pitched battles with the better-armed Turks. However, King Hussein, who was suspicious and jealous of al-Masri, was not convinced. The innovator was fired, but part of the core of his thinking was adopted and enlarged upon by Lawrence, working along parallel lines.

Lawrence came to the same general strategic conclusions as al-Masri, but refined them into a far subtler operational plan. The Hejaz railway ran north-south through Arabia and Syria, connecting Damascus to the province, passing through 800 miles of deserts and water-scarce hills. The trains were the only link to Ottoman rule in this part of the world, the bloodstream keeping alive the Turkish body politic in Arabia and Syria. It was the railway and not Medina that was the key to the situation.

All the Turkish stations along the line were protected by identical stone fortresses, each with an underground well and surrounded by barbed wire. Lawrence realized that the Turks stationed in them had made prisoners of themselves. If the railway was menaced, but not entirely destroyed, the Turks would have little excuse to evacuate Medina and their other stations along the line, though they would be effectively surrounded by a sea of Hashemite well-wishers and forced to defend a precarious 800 mile front.

This strategic situation played entirely to the strengths of the Bedu. As Lawrence observed, "A difference in character between the Turkish and Arab armies, is, the more you distribute the former the weaker they become, and the more you distribute the latter the stronger they become."[9]

Culturally, the Arabs had little corporate spirit or collective discipline; they were magnificent individualists. This was at once their strength and their weakness. By urging a fighting strategy based upon the organic realities of Arab culture, Lawrence had happened upon an enduring truth of not just warfare, but of nation building itself—to be successful, work with existing cultural realties, and not against them.

The Bedu were also in phenomenal physical shape; they could run or walk for hours over burning sand or jagged rock. Compared with the Turks, the Bedu had a far more intimate knowledge of the terrain they were fighting in, an unbeatable home field advantage. And the desert itself provided perhaps their single greatest strength. The Arab guerilla campaign resembled more a series of naval engagements than conventional land-based operations. The side with the greatest flexibility of movement was bound to win.

The Bedu, with camels that could easily travel 250 miles between watering stops in the cauldron of the Arabian summer inferno and carry six weeks of food with them to boot, had a range of approximately 1,000 miles in desert raids. Mobility became one of the Bedu's greatest advantages. The desert also provided a protected hinterland into which the Turks dare not enter; a strategic reality vitally necessary for any successful guerrilla campaign. It proved the ultimate sanctuary for Feisal's men. Range, speed, and political support: these were the basic ingredients underlying the Bedu's stirring accomplishments in the Arab Revolt.

Lawrence reasoned that if he could blow up trains along the Hejaz line without rendering the route irreparably damaged, he could physically tie his Turkish enemies to their protected fortresses, where they would be in control of less than one percent of Arabia, leaving the vast bulk of the territory free of Turkish influence. While the Turks hid behind their entrenchments, lacking all intelligence and mobility, Lawrence and his raiders would know exactly where the enemy was at all times.

The trump card throughout the campaign was that the British transport route in the Red Sea was impregnable, whereas the Turkish supply lines along the railway were vulnerable. The Turkish fortifications, Medina included, would be left to rot on the vine, increasingly unimportant, while the Arab Revolt went on around them. For it was the food supply that tied the Turks to the railway; in the end, the Turks in Medina were forced to eat their pack animals in order to survive. But the garrison played no further significant role in the fighting.

Between October and December 1917, Lawrence's Arab dynamiters destroyed 17 trains, spreading chaos along the Hejaz line. It was work for which the Bedu were well suited: it involved surprise, individual valor, superior understanding of the terrain, the propensity to loot and cause chaos, and the ability to speedily leave the scene. Lawrence, though never in charge of the Arab looting expeditions, believed in showing the Arabs he was with them through acts of great valor; by the end of the war, he had personally dynamited 23 bridges, although he later claimed that the number was higher.

While the possible rewards were great in terms of looting, so were the penalties; as has been true of most modern insurgencies, there were significant atrocities committed by the threatened ruling power. This was certainly true of the Ottoman Army, regarding its treatment of Arab captives. It was a primary reason why so few Arabs were taken prisoner by the Turks; everyone knew that killing one's wounded comrades was preferable to the horrific fate that awaited them.

After Aqaba, Allenby saw what a boon Lawrence's guerilla campaign was to his general strategy. The guerilla fighting proved a massive inconvenience for the Turks. Approximately 3,000 Bedu raiders effectively tied down around 50,000 Turkish soldiers, nearly 16 times their number. This was 50,000 Turks who were not able to either threaten Allenby's right flank or to critically reinforce their comrades when Allenby broke the Turkish lines in early fall 1918. If it is so that the Arabs could never have overthrown the Turks without British help, it also seems quite likely that the British would not have carried the day in theater if not for the Bedu and the masterful guerilla campaign devised by Lawrence.

Lawrence had initiated a highly successful guerrilla campaign, first in Arabia and later in Greater Syria, which stressed the importance of winning over the local peoples and making them stakeholders in the Arab Revolt for independence against the Turkish-dominated Ottoman Empire. But the revolt needed constant tending, for it was far from inevitable that the fragile flower of Arab unity would blossom.

To begin with, there were cultural problems. At moments of success in the guerilla campaign, when the battle was won and the Bedu, as was traditional, set about plundering their victims, the whole project would often come unhinged. As Lawrence explained, "a Bedouin force no longer exists when plunder has been obtained, since each man only cares to get off home with it."[10] The tribes served entirely on a voluntary basis; whenever they either had enough booty or were fed up taking orders from either the British or Feisal, they could simply leave. This meant that holding the Arab army together became Feisal and Lawrence's main concern.

Following his meeting with Allenby, Lawrence headed back for Arabia, landing in Jeddah. There intelligence sources in Cairo alerted him to the fact that Auda, the hero of the recent campaign, was considering defecting to the Turks in return for a handsome bribe, placing all that they had gained in peril. By August 4, 1917, Lawrence was back at the port, where he purchased a famous war camel named Ghazala and sped toward Auda's camp on the outskirts of the city. Auda brazenly denied the claims, saying that he had only pretended to go over to the Turks for money in order to gain intelligence of their future plans. But he did mention that he had not yet received a reward from the British for taking Aqaba, nor a significant supply of guns, as had been promised by Lawrence.

Lawrence put an end to the potential crisis by describing to Auda the British shipment of arms that would soon be unloaded at Aqaba and making it clear that Feisal would be extremely grateful for all of Auda's sacrifices. Until then, Lawrence offered Auda an advance on what he was sure Feisal would bestow. Lawrence kept the story of Auda's near-treachery to himself, but he had little doubt of the precariousness of the Arab Revolt. As the war in the desert progressed, he would grow weary of the Howeitat's ever-increasing and preposterous demands.

Also compounding the tendency toward disintegration was the open animosity many tribes had for each other. Laconically comparing conditions in Arabia to the Western Front, Lawrence explains, "Conduct of the war in France would have been harder if each division, almost each brigade, of our army had hated every other with a deadly hatred and fought when they met suddenly."[11] In Feisal's camp, the Billie, Juheima, and Harb tribes were all longstanding blood enemies; only the magnetic personality and undisputed position of the sherif bound them together.

British transfers of arms and money had been absolutely central to the continuing success of the Arab Revolt and a key element in keeping the tribes united. Feisal used British gold to pay his commanders, British food to feed his men, and British weapons to adequately arm them against the Turks. Beyond these basics, small groups of British specialists such as engineers, gunners, signalers, supply officers, artillery experts, armored car drivers, and airmen vitally kept the revolt on track.

The British Navy had also played a central role in the revolt's success, particularly in the early phases of the conflict, as the British-Arab forces made their way up the Red Sea ports on the Arabian Peninsula. Candidly, Feisal left Lawrence in no doubt that without adequate supplies of arms and money, even the most loyal of his followers would soon leave camp, despite the genuine respect the tribes felt for him personally.

But it is far too easy to dismiss the magic Feisal and Lawrence wove around the tribes as simply or even primarily a matter of money and arms. Captain Hubert Young, a close colleague of Lawrence's during the war, and often his critic, made this clear, saying that "Lawrence could not have done what he did without the gold, but no one else could have done it with ten times the amount."[12] In *Seven Pillars of Wisdom,* Lawrence famously observed a central cultural characteristic of the region, "In the East, persons were more trusted than institutions."[13] There is little doubt that Lawrence personally became a figure of great importance among the tribes comprising Feisal's legions.

Lawrence's easy familiarity with Arab culture made him popular with the Bedu fighters. While on the march, Lawrence would recite Arab poetry, sing Arab songs, and could hold his own with the best of them in spreading camp gossip, which often centered on tribal politics and family pedigrees. Each of his masters, the Arabs and the British, tended to look at the revolt from his own specific perspective. More than anything else, Lawrence was the pivot of the rebellion, the fulcrum that linked two very different peoples to a common cause.

Lawrence's ultimate ambition for his Arab comrades was more about politics than martial success, more about psychology than practical gains. He and Feisal were not merely fighting a war; they were crafting a nation.

It is important to always remember that history is not only made by impersonal historical forces; it is made by people. This is especially true of the Arab Revolt, where the specific personages of Lawrence and Feisal

miraculously held the squabbling, disparate, anarchic, Arab forces together, welding them into a victorious army. In the process of doing so,
they began to make that nation.

A key Lawrencian insight is that without Arab unity there would be
no ultimate capture of Damascus, historical symbol of past Arab greatness. And without Damascus there would be no viable independent
Arab nation to crown their successes at the war's end. For Lawrence,
the conflict had become a means to a very different end; building that
Arab nation. Lawrence's larger nation-building philosophy grew out of
the organic principles he observed under the tremendous stress and
strain of the fighting in the Great War of 1914–1918. His insights were
grounded in that most valuable and demanding of intellectual acade-
mies, practical experience.

Chapter 3

"There is a point where coddling becomes wicked."

—Lawrence, in a letter to Mrs. George Bernard Shaw, 1927

In August 1917, following the capture of Aqaba, the British High Command, fearing that Lawrence could be killed at any moment given the day-to-day perils he was exposed to and the risks that he was running spearheading the guerilla campaign, tasked him with codifying what he had learned about the Arabs in a manual that could be used by British officers serving in the field with Feisal's troops. It was rightly feared that if Lawrence were to die, his unique knowledge of dealing with the Arab forces would be forever lost. Cairo pressed him to name a successor in the field should he be killed; Lawrence unhelpfully, and only half-jokingly, suggested Gertrude Bell, given her vast knowledge of the desert and its people. So Lawrence, in the midst of the guerrilla campaign that followed Aqaba, wearily began typing his "Twenty-Seven Articles" in the heat of the desert sun.

The "Twenty-Seven Articles" is a brilliant mixture of political, military, and psychological thought, offering nothing less than a new way for Western nation-builders to look at the rest of the world. Decades ahead of his time, Lawrence realized that without the political backing of the local Arab population he could not win, and that with their support he could not lose.

Appearing in the *Arab Bulletin,* August 20, 1917, Lawrence makes clear that the 27 general rules he propounds are based on his experiences in Hejaz and therefore apply only to the Bedu. However, in fact what Lawrence laid out was a startlingly original general philosophy for nation building. He was not merely describing how to run a successful insurgency, though that would have been entirely sufficient; he was describing the principles involved in helping to create a nation.

Best of all, Lawrence thought and wrote about nation building in real time, as he was working with and fighting for the Arab cause. These are not the placid ruminations of some creaky scholar locked away in a cloister, but rather the day-to-day personal conclusions arrived at by a man of practical affairs, confronting the daily challenges of both holding the Arab army together and helping to transform that army into the vanguard of the Arab nationalist cause. A student of the classics, Lawrence would have known the Greek word for what he was aiming for: *praxis,* the unity of thought and action.

For Lawrence, local organic developments, specific cultural knowledge, and an emphasis on the particular are the keys to successful nation building. He stressed the conservative view of the nineteenth century Anglo-Irish philosopher Edmund Burke that politics is an organic construction; like a plant it grows out of the soil of a unique history, culture, and set of circumstances. Policy initiatives tend to work best when they are implemented in an organic, bottom-up manner, when they take account of indigenous realities, and when they work with the currents of history. Understanding and working with local culture and the politics that flow from it is what matters most. Tribe by tribe, village by village, Lawrence and Feisal, in both the Hejaz and Greater Syria, assembled a fighting force politically loyal to the Hashemites.

The second principle of the "Twenty-Seven Articles" states: "Learn all you can about your Ashraf and Bedu. Get to know their families, clans and tribes, friends and enemies, wells, hills, and roads."[1] Hans Morgenthau, an early pioneer in the study of international relations, later echoed Lawrence's emphasis on the power of local knowledge;[2] it is impossible to transform a society of which one knows precious little.

Amazingly, Lawrence's seemingly commonsensical view expressed in his report has always been a minority position from his own day until the present. During his era, the French were the leading exponents of a top-down form of colonial control. Lawrence hated the French style of governance because "the Frenchman held himself up as an example to be imitated: rather than learn Arabic, he encouraged the Arab to learn French; rather than learn Arab customs and traditions, he encouraged the Arab to ape his own."[3]

Today's America has almost wholly adopted this top-down approach that Lawrence so despised in its post–Cold War efforts at nation building. Lawrence's very contrary principles suggest that learning about the peoples one is attempting to help become stable societies is immediately more important than forcing them to accept Western norms that have played no historical role in their culture.

There are both general and specific practical policy advantages to such an approach. At the macro level, because they stressed the need to work entirely within the existing Arab social and political structure, Lawrence's policies had a real chance of taking root, of acquiring the indigenous support that makes policy longevity possible. Working with the grain of history contrasts with grafting foreign ideas onto a native culture, where, as in medicine and horticulture, such an intrusion is often rejected in quick order.

Such an approach makes local consensus, which is so vital for successful nation building, at least a possibility. As Lawrence pointed out in Article 23, "Experience of them [local peoples], and knowledge of their prejudices will enable you to foresee their attitude and possible course of action in nearly every case."[4] Understanding that Feisal and his sherifs viewed the events of the Great War through the lens of Arab culture enabled Lawrence to successfully influence Arab decision-making by working with, not against, Arab givens.

Lawrence was personally aware of what happens when a westerner takes charge of another people's destiny; he quickly gets out of his depth. During one guerrilla raid, Lawrence was forced to lead an expedition, rather than serve in his customary role of chief advisor to a sherif. He later ruefully remembered, "I had to be OC (officer in charge) of the whole expedition. This is not a job which should be undertaken by foreigners, since we have not so intimate a knowledge of Arab families . . . I had to adjudicate in twelve cases of assault with weapons, four camel-thefts, one marriage-settlement, fourteen feuds, two evil eyes, and a be-witchment. These affairs take up all one's spare time."[5] Even an Arab scholar such as Lawrence was bound to make serious mistakes given this daunting range of cultural decisions. How much more is this the case when local knowledge is almost entirely lacking, as occurred in American nation-building efforts in both Vietnam and Iraq.

It is measure of Lawrence's success in mastering the basics of Arab culture that it was Feisal himself who first suggested that he wear the robes of a sherif, which signified as nothing else could that the Arab tribesmen considered Lawrence "one of us." In fact, Feisal would be vexed on the rare occasions that Lawrence appeared in regulation British khaki, as if this somehow symbolized a breaking of faith with the honorary tribal membership that the Arabs had bestowed on him. Lawrence writes in Article 18 of the "Twenty-Seven Articles," "if you can wear Arab kit when with the tribes, you will acquire their trust and intimacy to a degree impossible in uniform."[6] Wearing Arab dress became the symbol of Lawrence's cultural understanding of and affinity for the Arab world, a metaphorical badge of his radical approach of working with the Bedu from a bottom-up perspective. The final point of the "Twenty-Seven Articles" is a summation: "The beginning and ending of the secret of handling Arabs is unremitting study of them."[7]

Although he had no formal military training, Lawrence had read his von Clausewitz. Like the great Prussian military theorist, Lawrence saw clearly that military strategies were formulated to achieve political outcomes, and not the other way around. The revolt was more about politics than military matters, more about culture than wherewithal, and more about psychology than weaponry. As Lawrence explained shortly after the war's end, "We had seldom to concern ourselves about what our men did, but much with what they thought."[8] In *Seven Pillars*, Lawrence acidly notes that until he arrived on the scene in Arabia, there had been "no attempt made to find out the local conditions and adapt existing Allied resources in material to suit their needs."[9]

A central tenet of the "Twenty-Seven Articles" is that to be effective, the Bedu must be permitted to fight as they always had done. To try to impose a British military style on the Arabs, to try to make them pale copies of British regular troops, was to doom them to defeat. Article 22 sternly warns British officers in Arabia not to "trade on what you know of fighting. The Hejaz confounds ordinary tactics. Learn the Bedu principles of war as thoroughly and as quickly as you can . . . Do not waste Bedu attacking trenches [they will not stand casualties]."[10] Lawrence understood that the Bedu were great fighters, but not in a conventional Western sense. As he wrote in the British newspaper the *Times,* "The Bedouin is hostile to discipline, and unfit for regular service; though on his own day, in his own country, and in his own style, he will dispose of many times his number of any troops that can be brought against him."[11]

The Bedu actually presented their British allies with organic advantages. With their far greater mobility, a product of the Bedu nomadic lifestyle that had remained unchanged for generations, Feisal's army could operate independently of bases, where it was beyond the power of their Turkish adversaries to follow. By adapting guerilla strategy to Bedu traditional warfare tactics, Lawrence and Feisal's men could harass the Turks, sever their lines of communication, all while avoiding the decisive set-piece battles so beloved of the British.

Lawrence also understood that local Arab politics superseded whatever was happening militarily. In fact, the military outcome of the revolt would be largely dependent on the political disposition of the locals. As Lawrence observes in "Twenty-Seven Articles," the key to victory was simple—gain local civilian sympathy. For the Arab Revolt to succeed, "It must have a friendly population not actively friendly, but sympathetic to the point of not betraying rebel movements to the enemy. Rebellions can be made by 2 percent active in a striking force, and 98 percent passively sympathetic."[12]

Centrally, Lawrence never forgot that for Feisal and the Arabs the ultimate goal of the war was political: to forge an Arab nation. For nation building to be successful, determining the local unit of politics is the key; in the case of the Arabs it was the fiercely independent tribe and not the Western preference of some Jeffersonian construct.

Then, as now, there were enormous differences between types of Arabs; they were and are not a unified religious or ethnic group. For example, the Bedu tribesmen of the Hejaz had little in common with the urban populations of Aleppo, Dera, and Damascus in Greater Syria. The three main commonalities of the Arab world in Lawrence's day constituted only a slender reed of sameness—they were Islam, (though it too is far more heterogeneous than outsiders imagine); language (though Arab dialects vary greatly); and a shared pride in their glorious history. The one characteristic that all the Bedu tribes did tend to share made Lawrence and Feisal's efforts at nation building almost impossible; it was their fierce independence. The Bedu recognized no higher authority than local control. (It is easy to see Lawrence's affinity for the Bedu; like him they were eminently not clubbable.) Lawrence's challenge was to make a stable nation of tribesmen who did not believe in nationalism in a Western sense.

Lawrence squared this circle by working with Arab political realities, and not ignoring them. The unit of politics in the Bedu world was tribal and local, whether he liked it or not. As he made clear, "There is no national feeling. Between town and town, village and village, family and family, creed and creed, exist intricate jealousies, sedulously fostered by the Turks to render a spontaneous union impossible. The largest indigenous political entity in settled Syria is only the village under its sheikh, and in patriarchal Syria the tribe under its chief."[13] Rather than ignore this inconvenient fact, Lawrence chose to work with it as a political reality, building a sense of Arab nationhood from the ground up, constructing it on the basis of the genuine organic cultural and political characteristics of the Bedu.

In this, long-standing Turkish over-lordship actually helped the cause. Because of centuries of relatively weak Ottoman rule, the Arabs possessed a great deal of practical control over their own affairs. This sustained the Arab belief that one's primary loyalty was to the local political institutions of the tribe and the village. Brilliantly, Lawrence understood that such a fractured political reality called for the "minimum of central power,"[14] as confederation organically meshed with the strong localism that defined Arab politics in Feisal's army as well as in Greater Syria. Lawrence, knowing his Bedu comrades, could see that less government for them was better, as it suited their lifestyle as well as their intrinsic political view of the world.

To impose a political system from outside that does not correspond to local political realities is to create an artificial state, and to fail at nation building. Lawrence's great insight was to properly perceive that the tribe and the village was the Arab unit of politics, and then to work with the grain of history, proposing the political system of confederation that actually fit this reality on the ground. Tailoring a system to fit the local political unit of politics, rather than imposing a one-size-fits-all overly centralized system on indigenous peoples, is a major insight Lawrence has to teach the would-be nation-builders of today.

Lawrence was acutely aware that, as an outsider, he had to appear to be above local politics; he could not be seen to be in the business of picking local winners and losers. As Feisal's primary British representative, he knew that his personal favor or disfavor of particular Arab leaders would be used by local elites to discredit those he sided with. They would quickly be accused of being imperial stooges, lackeys of the

British government, which would cost them their local legitimacy. Ironically, by making his support known, Lawrence would be doing a disservice to the leaders he liked, undermining their effectiveness with their people.

Rather like a sherif, Lawrence stood aloof from any one tribe or tribal leader, making it clear that he served wholly at the behest of emir Feisal, who came to epitomize greater Arab unity. Lawrence operationalized this key philosophical stance by making it a point to serve on guerrilla raids with many different tribes, never becoming militarily associated with any one group of Bedu or their leaders. As Article 8 clearly urges: "Avoid being identified too long or too often with any tribal sheikh, even if CO [Commanding Officer] of the expedition . . . Sherifs are above all blood-feuds and local rivalries, and form the only principle of unity among the Arabs. Let your name therefore be coupled always with a Sherif's, and share his attitude toward the tribes."[15] Because he understood both Arab psychology and individual tribal politics, Lawrence was able to navigate the treacherous shoals of inter-Bedu politics.

This contrasts mightily with post–Cold War efforts at nation building, where local leaders are invariably viewed as being either pro-Western or enemies of the nation-building exercise itself. It never seems to dawn on modern day nation-builders that by bestowing favor on local leaders, they are often limiting their effectiveness. For one of the few political sentiments that seems to be universal is the desire not to be told what to do by outside forces, or have leaders who bow to such forces' will. As staunch believers in nationalism and localism, outsiders would do well to remember that other peoples have similar motivations. By being seen as too close to possible local allies, modern nation builders often bestow the kiss of death on their indigenous political legitimacy. This was a reality that Lawrence understood well and successfully steered clear of.

Perhaps most importantly of all, Lawrence believed that nation-building would not succeed unless it was advanced by the locals themselves. In *Seven Pillars,* Lawrence makes it clear that the Arab Revolt "was an Arab war waged and led by Arabs for an Arab aim in Arabia."[16] He makes explicit the revolt's larger political goal—that through the trial by fire of the Great War, the Arabs had largely liberated themselves and as such were due an independent self-governing state. If the British were seen as being forced to primarily fight Arab battles for them, Feisal and his family would have little claim to nationhood at the end of the war for independence.

For moral reasons, but also for practical ones, indigenous peoples must be made primary stakeholders in nation-building efforts. Working with leaders with genuine local legitimacy is central to the process, and above all the West should help but not dictate, facilitate but not dominate, influence but not run, advise but not manage. The differences in these terms are not semantic. They denote wholly different approaches to nation building. Whereas the West has always adopted a more active role for itself in nation building, Lawrence preferred the subtler intellectual approach, critically reserving the first place for local leaders in the story of their own national regeneration. For Lawrence it was self-evident that failing this, nation-building efforts would not prove self-sustaining.

Lawrence had recognized this truth almost from the beginning. When the revolt was at its lowest ebb, just as he became involved in the desert campaign well before Aqaba, he had strenuously opposed the policy put forward by many in Cairo of wholesale British involvement in Arabia. It was thought, as the dominant power in the relationship, British forces alone could save the sputtering Arab Revolt. Lawrence knew that this would amount to a British takeover; de facto Feisal's small army would cease to play an independent role in their own war of liberation from the Turks.

Instead, Lawrence urged that British advisors—specialists to man the machine guns, fly the planes, and competently deliver supplies—join Feisal's troops, rather than British troops engaging *en masse.* For if thousands of British troops were allowed free rein in the land of the holy places of Islam, it would forever discredit both Feisal and Hussein, who would be seen by their people as cravenly willing to profane their duties as the custodians of Mecca and Medina in order to help their British allies; non-believers (in this case non-Muslims) were not to be present in large numbers in the land of Islam's holy sites. If this were to occur, the Hashemites would be viewed as puppets of the British Empire, and the revolt would lose all local legitimacy. Lawrence saw both the threat of over-involvement by the British, as well as the opportunity that Arab self-help could play in their own nation-building efforts.

Vitally, Lawrence understood that local legitimacy was the key to stability in the Middle East. Feisal, as leader of the Bedu, was the personal expression of this political truth. Though he was short, soft-spoken, and shy, even as a young man the shrewd Feisal was a force to be reckoned with. As the son of Emir Hussein, the keeper of the Muslim holy places of Mecca and Medina, Feisal enjoyed the religious legitimacy this conveyed upon his Hashemite family. In addition, Feisal was, uniquely, acceptable to the loosely aligned tribes of the Arabian Desert and Greater Syria: the Rwalla, the Serahin, the Bani Sakhr, and the Howeitat. Not only had Feisal given them victory (not a small consideration in Arab culture), he also spoke their dialect of Arabic, understood their tribal structure, and knew their histories.

In short, Feisal had the critical advantage of political legitimacy, based on shared cultural ties with his men. Lawrence, from their fateful first meeting in Hamra in Arabia in 1916, had recognized the central role Feisal must play if the revolt was to prove successful. He saw his own role as advisory. As he stressed in Article 3 of the "Twenty-Seven Articles," "Never give orders to anyone at all . . . Your place is advisory, and your advice is due to the commander alone. Let him see this is your conception of your duty, and that his is to be the sole executive of your joint plans."[17] Article 11 continues in this vein: "Wave a Sherif in front of you like a banner and hide your own mind and person."[18] During the war, all major military operations Lawrence participated in were at least nominally led by an Arab commander-in-chief, with Lawrence in a vital but supporting role, as advisor.

In Article 14 Lawrence links his cultural understanding of the Bedu to exercising power. "While very difficult to drive, the Bedu are easy to lead, if you have the patience to bear with them. The less apparent your interferences, the more your influence."[19] Lawrence was translating his medieval expertise, based more on having the indirect influence of a courtier rather than the seemingly unlimited powers of a twentieth century pro-counsel, into a practical strategy for the modern world.

Lawrence's philosophy was not the product of a Western plot; it was not a more sophisticated way of fooling the Arabs into a more nuanced form of submission. Rather it amounts to a far more thoughtful and very different way of westerners working with developing peoples, a philosophy that had at least had the potential to serve the interests of both. For Lawrence, Western influence over the Bedu had to be grounded in genuine cultural understanding of the people with which he was working.

Such realities extend to the modern world. The only genuine positive political development in post-Saddam Iraq has been "The Awakening" movement of disaffected Sunnis against the barbaric degradations of al-Qaeda in Iraq. The alienated Sunni tribes organically rose up to put an end to the foreign imposition of al-Qaeda. General Petraeus and his troops did not create this movement, but rather successfully took advantage of what was an organic, local development, working with and arming the locals, who far more effectively began to turn the tide in Iraq against foreign terrorists. It is little surprise that this positive political development was almost entirely home grown, with the U.S. military under General Petraeus playing an important, but thoroughly secondary, role.

As at Carchemish, in Arabia, Lawrence's goal was to enable Arab men to do their own work better. As he wrote to his confidante and adopted mother figure, Charlotte Shaw, the wife of playright George Bernard Shaw, after the war, "All of my experience of the Arabs was of the God-father role. My object . . . was always to make them stand on their own feet."[20] For Lawrence simply wanted to help the Arabs help themselves.

Lawrence's philosophy was tested in the most unforgiving classroom imaginable; the real world engulfed in the horrors of global war. Lawrence's friend and biographer, the writer Robert Graves, estimated that the British government spent around 10 million pounds on the Arab Revolt, and endured a score or so of British casualties in fighting alongside Feisal. It was Lawrence's brilliant, if unorthodox, philosophy that made British expenditure a bargain at this price.

Lawrence's philosophy also possesses a foreign policy aspect. To maintain real power within the British sphere of influence, it was best to assist and not manage other nations. As such, the sooner Britain turned over local administration to its colonies, making them dominions, the better. Much as this had proven true locally, within Bedu society, it is also critical at the national level.

After the war, Lawrence devised a global plan for the British Empire that complemented the micro-level view of the "Twenty-Seven Articles." In a 1920 article on "The New Imperialism," published anonymously in the British journal the *Round Table,* he sets out a continuation of his philosophy, adding a novel way to manage nation building at the colonial level, as well as a new geopolitical strategy for the British Empire.

Lawrence had laid out his strategy in a letter to the arch-imperialist conservative foreign minister, Lord Curzon: "My own ambition is that the Arabs should be our first brown Dominion, and not our last brown colony."[21] Calling his approach "the New Imperialism," Lawrence envisioned London pulling back from its colonies, adopting an advisory rather than a governing role. For example, Lawrence urged that the Arabs be allowed to run their own domestic affairs, while ceding control of their defense and foreign policy to London, much as Australia, South Africa, and New Zealand had done pre-1914.

What is striking is how closely Lawrence's "new imperialism" mirrors the earlier "Twenty-Seven Articles" in its emphasis on the counterintuitive idea that ceding local control was in the best interests of Britain. "This New Imperialism is not just withdrawal or neglect on

our part. It involves an active side of imposing responsibility on the
local peoples. It is what they clamor for, but an unpopular gift when
given . . . We can only teach them by forcing them to try, while we stand
by and give advice. This is not for us less honorable than administration:
indeed, it is more exacting, for it is simple to give orders, but difficult
to persuade another to take advice."[22] Local governments, like individuals, should be pressed to stand on their own. Only peoples and governments in charge of their own destiny, possessing local legitimacy, are
likely to prove successful.

In terms of policy, and in opposition to the modern, top-down efforts of Paul Bremer in Iraq, Lawrence stressed that the Middle Eastern
rulers must have their own army and police force as soon as proved practical, as a symbol to their people that there was indigenous control of the
most basic of a state's functions: to guarantee the order of their nation.
Only by thrusting the demanding day-to-day realities of governing onto
indigenous leaders with local legitimacy, could genuine progress in nation building take place.

Just as Lawrence's domestic approach to nation building demands
an entirely different mindset, so his colonial and geopolitical strategy required western states, in this case Britain, to radically think again about
the relationship between their country and the developing world. To
achieve organic and enduring progress on the ground, he felt the British
must change their role in their colonies from "decider" to "advisor," not
an easy thing to ask of an imperial power that is used to giving orders.
Aware that it required a psychological adjustment, Lawrence urges in the
Round Table article, "We have to be prepared to see them doing things
by methods quite unlike our own, and less well: but on principle it is
better that they half-do it than that we do it perfectly for them."[23] For

Lawrence, the key measure of nation building was who did the constructing, far more than the immediate results.

Finally, at the geostrategic level, Lawrence urges that by decentralizing power the great powers stood to gain more political support than by rigidly demanding obedience of weaker states. In terms of enhancing alliance management, by making stakeholders of an enlarged commonwealth of allies, Lawrence hoped to perpetuate declining British power.

Lawrence was not alone in his opinions. The *Round Table* magazine, where Lawrence first put forward his policy of the new imperialism, pushed the idea that, with the shock of the Great War just behind it, the British Empire must either federate, diffusing power to some extent, or disintegrate. Lawrence merely added the notion that the Arabs should be part of this push toward increased political status for the British dominions, such as Australia, Canada, South Africa, and New Zealand.

For the British core to survive as a Great Power, it was obvious to men such as Lawrence that these peripheries, if they were to remain part of the British world, must have a greater say in their own political arrangements. He saw this approach as a way to harness the geopolitical potential of the Middle East to the declining might of London. He urged that "Egypt, Persia and Mesopotamia [Iraq], if assured of eventual dominion status, and present internal autonomy, would be delighted to affiliate with us, and would then cost us no more in men and money than Canada and Australia."[24] Counter-intuitively, Lawrence believed that further integrating the troublesome Arab world into the British Empire would turn the restive peoples of the Middle East, having been granted the autonomy they pleaded for, into stalwart defenders of the British imperial order.

After the Great War, as is now increasingly true for the United States under Barack Obama, Britain found itself first among equals in the global order, but in relative decline, surrounded by a world of rapidly rising powers. As structurally the United States. finds itself in an eerily similar position to Lawrence's Britain, his lessons for alliance management seem as relevant for Washington today as they were for London in the early 1920s.

For all his brilliance as a soldier and a man of action, it is Lawrence's role as a thinker ahead of his time that is most valuable for the world we live in. Lawrence's forgotten philosophy, with an intellectual reach well beyond the immediate specifics and place of the Arab Revolt and the time of the Great War, points to a very different strategy of nation building from the top-down failures we see today. The story of what happened to both the man and his ideas lies ahead of us; but so, perhaps, does the resurrection of his thought.

Chapter 4

"My dreams puffed out like candles, in the strong wind of success."

—Lawrence on the political outcome in Damascus, October 1918

By the summer of 1918, during the latter stages of the Syrian guerrilla campaign, Lawrence was beginning to exhibit signs of advanced psychological strain. In early September 1918, he was slightly wounded by a bomb fragment. His prided-upon indifference to pain gone, Lawrence burst into tears, where earlier and more significant injuries had left him unmoved. Plagued by chronic insomnia, and with his weight down to 80 pounds from his usual 112, he was exhausted and depressed, and well on his way to a mental breakdown, even as he neared the gates of Damascus.

By the fall of 1918, Feisal was also at the end of his tether. Plagued by his envious father, who resented his growing reputation, the prince resigned as the designated leader of the revolt in a fit of frustration. Hashemite officers had read a news report in which Hussein denied that Jafar Pasha, commander of the revolt's Northern Army, had ever been appointed to the position. In reality, this was Hussein's last pathetic effort to assert control over Feisal, who had personally advanced Jafar in 1917, without consulting his jealous father.

On hearing of the report and smarting at the lack of confidence it implied, Jafar and his officers resigned. Feisal followed suit, in a gesture that was both directed against his father and as a symbol of his solidarity with the Arab officers who had taken the revolt so far. On the eve of victory, the dream of Arab unity looked likely to collapse into petty bickering.

In a panic and knowing that literally there was no one who could take Feisal's place, Lawrence prevailed upon Emir Hussein to write his son a telegram to patch things up. The stubborn old man grudgingly complied. It was just enough. Lawrence, intercepting the message ahead of Feisal, decoded for him only the first portion, which was conciliatory, rather than the whole of it, which was less gracious. Feisal, still wounded by his father's lack of gratitude for his efforts, retook command of the revolt.

However, the schism between father and son had permeated the ranks of the tribes, just as victory was upon them. While the Arab Revolt continued, an adequate degree of discipline was never restored. It was not just Lawrence who was coming undone; so was the political leadership of his army. Arab unity was undoubtedly real, but it certainly remained a fragile thing.

This disintegration was also evident in a number of events occurring as the war drew to what should have amounted to a glorious climax. During the race toward Damascus, in the summer of 1918, Auda, ever the cantankerous brigand, commandeered a load of supplies designed for the revolt, and refused to release them unless Lawrence paid a ransom of 10,000 pounds in gold. Lawrence quickly met Auda's demands, and downplayed the incident to the point that he did not include it in his account of the final stages of the war in *Seven Pillars of Wisdom*. This made sound public relations sense; if the world was to see that Auda and the tribes were not selfless knights but instead were often very much self-interested, anarchic bandits, the Arab cause could well suffer a mortal blow in terms of global opinion.

The ungluing of the Arab army was also apparent on the battlefield. On September 27, 1918, with the Ottoman army in full retreat and the British and Arabs driving on Damascus, the retreating Turks gathered the villagers of Tafas, and then raped, tortured, and mutilated the women, while massacring the men and children; there were no survivors. When Lawrence and the Arab army came upon the scene of the slaughter, the Turkish soldiers, with their German allies, were just pulling out of the town. The Arab leader of the village, Talal, had been prominent in the revolt and was a personal friend of Lawrence's. Overcome with despair and rage, he did what was expected of him in the Arab honor culture: he suicidally charged alone on horseback into the retreating Turkish column, to avenge his fallen kinsmen. He was shot down just short of the Ottoman lines.

Watching all this, Auda cried, "We will take his price,"[1] urging the Arab irregulars into the disorganized Turks. Lawrence, disgusted by what he had seen in Tafas, where the Turks had killed babies and obscenely mutilated the women of the village (Lawrence saw a pregnant woman dead with a bayonet between her legs), called for no prisoners to be taken. The Arab forces fell on the disorganized and terrified Ottomans and their German allies, slaughtering them.

After the brief and barbaric fight was at an end, Lawrence came upon a victim of the Turkish war crimes, an Arab soldier whose shoulder had been pinned to the ground by a bayonet. When Lawrence asked who had done this to him, the solider pointed to the 250 Turkish prisoners that had just been taken; they were machine-gunned to death. While the Arab rage was certainly understandable, Tafas illustrates the decline not just of Arab discipline, but also Lawrence's personal deterioration. Feisal's troops, with Lawrence present and in some form of control, had participated in what in modern terms can only be described as a crime of retribution for Turkish atrocities. These events, alongside the Arab looting that was to take place in Damascus itself, reveal an army and a leadership coming apart at the seams.

But by far the biggest crisis looming on the horizon had to do with British political duplicity. For in the life-and-death desperation of World War I, Britain had offered the same parcel of land in the Middle East to two different allies, the Arabs and the French. As Lawrence drove on Damascus in the late summer and early of fall of 1918, this contradiction began to tear at both him and the Arab army, lurking just beneath the surface of things.

The narrative of British promises and half-promises is a tangled tale. It begins in 1915 with inducements offered by Sir Henry McMahon, then British high commissioner in Cairo, to King Hussein, hoping to persuade him to rise up against the Ottomans. The McMahon-Hussein secret correspondence came to a climax on October 24, 1915, when McMahon wrote that an Arab rising would lead Britain to recognize Arab independence throughout the region, "except where Britain is not free to act to the detriment of France."[2]

This giant loophole is beyond vague, perfectly preserving British diplomatic freedom of movement about the geographical boundaries of any new Arab state. For the British, in reality, had not promised much of anything. France, with its claims to the same parcel of the Middle East as the Hashemites, were always going to be the sticking point in any diplomatic deal. The British had remained entirely non-committal about this crucial point. Hussein accepted these vague but broadly encouraging terms.

The Sykes-Picot Agreement of February 1916 was a far more precise exercise. Signed by Britain, France, and Russia, it amounted to an imperial carve-up of the Middle East, on the lines of a standard nineteenth century exercise of imperial power. France was to get parts of the Lebanese and Syrian coast, with the Arabs gaining control of the Syrian hinterlands, along the Aleppo-Damascus line, east to Mosul, in what is today's Kurdish region of Iraq.

The treaty was in clear conflict with the promises McMahon had made to Hussein, effectively implying that France would dominate the whole of Arab territory; it would control all the ports of Syria, possessing an effective economic stranglehold on the newborn Arab state. In addition, the Arab government would be saddled with French advisers, who would play a large and unspecified role in Syria's governance. Given France's notorious preference for top-down imperial control, it is clear that what the imperial powers had in mind was the creation of a weak, Arab puppet state, dominated by France.

Under the terms of the agreement, Czarist Russia was finally to get control of the strategic Dardanelles straits from Turkey. Beyond Arabia, which was reserved for King Hussein, Britain was to get much of what was left, including Mesopotamia and Palestine. The fact that the agreement was kept secret was a sign that even its authors in Paris and London knew the publication of such a cynical document would be harmful to the war effort.

The secret agreement was made public in October 1917, following the Russian Revolution, when the Bolsheviks gleefully published all the secret treaties of the capitalist powers in the newspaper *Izvestia*. Its unearthing was a dagger pointed at the heart of the British war effort in the Middle East. The British knew that one thing was not in doubt. The motive behind the Arab Revolt was their genuine belief that they would have a truly independent state after the war had come to an end. Without the possibility that this dream would be fulfilled, the rebellion was certain to peter out.

London's contradictory promises to the Arabs and the French made Sykes-Picot the diplomatic context for the tension in British policy in the Middle East during the latter stages of the war. Faced with the greatest threat to its existence since Napoleon, Britain needed both French and Arab help at the same time; the necessity of victory would allow Britain the luxury to deal with such problems later, but victory was first essential.

Hussein had been privately informed of the treaty's broad contents by its two main authors—Sir Mark Sykes of Britain and Monsieur Georges Picot of France—in May 1917. What they said to the aging king is not precisely known. The Arab interpretation is that they simply lied to him, saying that Sykes-Picot was merely a draft of a Franco-British agreement that had never been ratified.

Feisal knew about Sykes-Picot, but was never officially informed of its terms; his British allies never deigned to brief him. Instead the prince got second-hand information through his father. When Feisal contacted his father for clarification, the old man assured him that all was well. Feisal later remembered, "King Hussein communicated to London and the British Government assured him that the sensational news reported by the Turks (who had translated the *Izvestia* report into Arabic) was merely an intrigue on their part, and that England had no interest other than that of the liberation of all the Arabs."[3] This was either a misunderstanding, or, more likely, a deliberate falsehood. It had the desired effect of keeping the Arab army in the field.

However, the Turks sensed an opening. By now fearing that they would lose both the war and their Arabian possessions, they seized the diplomatic opportunity and began making overtures to Feisal, whispering of British treachery. Feisal, like the British, was keeping his options open. Until June 1918, he was secretly in negotiations with Jamal Pasha, the Turkish ruler of Greater Syria, regarding a possible separate settlement of the revolt. Lawrence knew of this dallying, having bribed one of Feisal's secretaries and seen the Feisal-Jamal correspondence. He was well aware the revolt was hanging by a thread.

As *Seven Pillars* makes clear, the only way Lawrence could square the contradiction of his serving two masters was to see himself as capable of balancing Arab and British interests, which was possible only as long as he felt that they were complementary. Obviously, this would only prove true if Arab independence, and not Sykes-Picot, became the dominant policy of the British Empire. Motivated by guilt, and the unalterable British social rule that a gentleman pays his debts, Lawrence took it as his personal responsibility to scupper the Sykes-Picot agreement and ensure that Feisal became king of Greater Syria.

In January 1918, Feisal had urgently asked Lawrence to get the British cabinet to disavow the recently published Sykes-Picot. This was the first of Lawrence's several attempts to clarify British intentions. He was met by more British duplicity. Then, in early June, the British War Cabinet's Middle Eastern Committee recommended a revision of Sykes-Picot, saying that changes in the circumstances of the war made its original terms unworkable. Partly, too, the times had simply changed. With the rise of both Woodrow Wilson in the United States and Lenin in Russia, anti-imperialist sentiment was gathering momentum around the world; Wilson, in particular, was gaining world-wide acclaim for calling for a peace without vindictiveness, in which the old nineteenth-century rules of imperial "property swaps" among the victors would be replaced by the principles of self-determination.

The earlier carve-up seemed increasingly shabby after so much suffering. Rightly nervous that the publication of Sykes-Picot might drive the Arabs into the arms of the waiting Turks, the British felt that soft words were necessary to keep the Arabs on side.

Finally, on June 16, 1918, the British government made a formal declaration of its policy in the Middle East. London recognized "the complete and sovereign independence" of all those "territories liberated from Turkish rule by the Arabs themselves."[4] Both Feisal and his father saw this "Declaration to the Seven," which was ostensibly written to placate the concerns of a group of seven Syrian nationalists, as a definitive repudiation of the earlier Sykes-Picot Agreement, a view that was strongly reinforced by Lawrence. Ominously, the French had yet to ratify the British changes to their common diplomatic position as Allenby neared Damascus in the summer of 1918. Yet, if he did not exactly know better, Lawrence suspected the coming betrayal of his Arab comrades. As the war wound down, the British and the French, in response to the great rhetorical pressure being exerted by their new American ally, Woodrow Wilson, veered ever further into diplomatic misdirection.

On November 9, 1918, just before the defeat of Germany, the British foreign office undersecretary, Lord Robert Cecil, published a further Anglo-French statement on the Middle East. In line with the Declaration to the Seven, and contradicting Sykes-Picot, it stated that Paris and London encouraged the establishment of native governments in Syria and Mesopotamia, and would not interfere in the workings of any local government. Then prime minister, David Lloyd George, in his book, *Memoirs of the Peace Conference,* includes the official Foreign Office translation of the pledge. "The goal aimed at by France and Great Britain in their conduct in the East of a war unchained by German ambition is the complete and definitive freedom of the peoples so long oppressed by the Turks, and the establishment of national governments and administrations deriving their authority from the initiative and free choice of the native population."[5]

The document continues, "Far from wishing to impose on the populations of these regions such or such institutions, they [Britain and France] have no other care than to assure by their support and practical aid the normal working of the governments and institutions which these populations have freely set up."[6]

Words matter, and these ought to pretty much put to rest the notion that the tragedy that was about to ensue was the result of some sort of grand linguistic misunderstanding. Rather, the British and the French understood all too well the game they were playing.

Still, Lawrence continued to press his government for clarification. In September 1918, he asked his friend and superior in Cairo, Colonel Clayton, head of the Arab Bureau, for further assurances.

Clayton blithely reassured Lawrence that Sykes-Picot could be forgotten. Indeed, at about the same time, British Foreign Minister Arthur Balfour told Allenby that the Hashemites had the right to hoist their flag over Damascus, if they got there first, in line with the most recent British diplomatic declarations. In turn, Allenby, on September 25, 1918, told Lawrence that he had no objections to an Arab advance on Damascus and their taking the city. The race for Damascus was on.

With the war in the Middle East fast approaching a climax while the global outcome was still very much in doubt—as late as the summer of 1918 the Germans pushed ahead with the massive "Kaiser's Battle" offensive on the Western Front—the British needed the help of the French and the Arabs more than ever; their own equivocation and, indeed, outright lying were the least of their worries. With the Arabs playing an important part in Allenby's drive on Damascus and with the French vital in the West, the most important strategic front of the war, British policy consisted of being seen as all things to all men.

However, in allowing Feisal to raise his standard over Damascus if he got there first, London, like Lawrence, seemed to be hoping that facts on the ground would dissuade the French from pursuing their claims to Greater Syria under the terms of Sykes-Picot. It was a gross misreading of French foreign policy intentions. France was determined, under Prime Minister Georges Clemenceau, to exact the maximum geopolitically for its horrid losses on the battlefield. The British, in the end, were reduced to a policy of hoping that somehow everything would simply work out, that the all these contrary demands could be reconciled. It was less a genuine strategy than a forlorn hope, born out of the exigencies of total war.

Allenby's big push began on September 19, 1918. Lawrence's Arabs, comprising the right of Allenby's overall force, were to seize the village of Dera, the main rail terminus south of Damascus. By cutting off the railway, they would prevent Turkish reinforcements from the south from supporting the main Turkish force after Allenby had struck the Ottoman center and left. Then, if possible, Lawrence and the Arabs were to move on Damascus itself.

For the final thrust, the Arabs assembled some 450 regulars under Nasir and Nuri Said along with 4,000 Bedu, 3,000 of whom were Rwalla tribesman, under Nuri Shalaan. The force was constantly being augmented as Lawrence headed north, as the Rwalla rose in fragmented fashion as he neared their individual villages. The ubiquitous Auda and his Howeitat were also there to be in at the kill, along with the Bani Sakhr, Serahin, and Ageyl, comprising the final 1,000 warriors.

It was a formidable display of troop strength, but the Arab army was still utterly dependent on British largesse; British money and supplies remained crucial. For the final offensive, Cairo had supplied Feisal with 700 camels, 300,000 pounds in gold for more recruitment along the way, and they promised him artillery and machine guns. Another British allocation, a Rolls Royce armored car, was used extensively by Lawrence himself. Capable of both great speed and mobility, armored cars were able to come up on isolated groups of Turks, taking them by complete surprise. They proved to be a critical technological innovation during the revolt's final stage. Lawrence named his car the Blue Mist; it held the extraordinary record of breaking down only once, despite many crossings over the wildest terrain imaginable.

But it was not just wherewithal that led to the Arab army's stunning triumph. Rather, the resoundingly successful final push to Damascus signaled, more than anything, the ultimate vindication of Lawrence's revolutionary philosophy. Lawrence's vast knowledge of Syrian tribes and geography, learned during his idyllic time at Carchemish, proved invaluable, particularly in recruiting the powerful Rwalla.

As Lawrence recounts in *Seven Pillars,* "Feisal's movement made the enemy country [Syria] friendly to the Allies as they advanced, enabling convoys to go up without escort, towns to be administered without garrison."[7] Despite longstanding Turkish control of Syria, it was the Arab revolt, and not the Ottoman forces, that had gained local sympathy, which allowed Lawrence and the Arab army to quickly advance over large swathes of territory without fretting about the political leanings of the local population.

Once Allenby smashed the Turkish line, its cohesion fell to pieces across the front. Ferociously harried by the Arabs (with Auda's Howeitat proving particularly adept at ambushes), Turkish stragglers were mercilessly cut down. After Dera fell, six Turkish regiments fell back toward Damascus. In the end, only a few shocked individuals actually reached the capital. The Arab force effectively destroyed what was left of the Ottoman Fourth Army.

Given stunning success of the Damascus campaign, there is plenty of credit to go around. Allenby's brilliant strategic plan allowed the British and their Arab allies to advance on Damascus, crossing 550 miles, traversing some of the most rugged and inhospitable terrain imaginable, shattering Ottoman resistance. During the campaign, the combined Turkish-German command lost over 100,000 soldiers due to fighting or disease, and an equal number were captured. Allenby lost a comparatively paltry 5,000 men.

There is no doubt that the Arab contribution to the final push to Damascus was significant. Of the 150,000 Turkish troops in theater, the Arabs killed an estimated 10,000. By the time of the final campaign in the Fall of 1918, it was being argued that the Hejaz Revolt directly occupied a vital 38,000 Ottoman soldiers, who were desperately needed elsewhere to shore up the sagging Turkish lines

Despite his suspicions about British intentions, Lawrence saw that the Damascus campaign provided a real chance for the Arabs to best their devious British and French allies. He feared that if General Sir Edmund Allenby's main army reached Damascus ahead of him, Britain would be forced to uphold the Sykes-Picot Agreement and turn the city over to France. But, if the Arabs got there first, fighting their way into the city, it might just persuade the French to accept a territorial concession elsewhere, as such an outcome would bolster Britain's contradictory declaration to the Arabs of June 1918.

The Arab leadership had no illusions about the politics underwriting Lawrence's lunge toward Damascus. Lawrence had written in a dispatch to Cairo in early February 1918 that Feisal, "says always that neither England nor France nor Turkey will give over to the Arabs one foot of unconquered ground, but that each new village occupied, each new tribe enrolled by Arab effort, is one more step forward towards the Arab State."[8]

In fact, "losing" the race to Damascus served British interests. As a practical matter, it made sound military sense for the Arabs to reach Damascus first. On September 29, 1918 it was decided at Allenby's field headquarters that Feisal's legions should be the only allied troops to initially occupy Damascus, presumably to forestall possible local resistance to a Christian occupation of the ancient Arab capital. Such an outcome would have the added advantage of letting the British off the very embarrassing diplomatic hook of having to own up to their duplicity and choose between wartime comrades.

But the race had to look genuine to the outside world, particularly to the French. That the British were stage-managing the effort can be deduced from the fact that the British advance guard from Allenby's main force, the Australian Mounted Division, under the command of Sir Henry Chauvel, was given explicit orders not to enter Damascus on September 30 unless forced to, even though they were slightly nearer the city than was Lawrence and the Arab army. Lawrence was to play the part of the pawn in a much larger British diplomatic game.

With the Turks put to flight, all that remained was for Lawrence and the Arab army to realize their unbelievable dream of taking the Arab symbol of its past greatness, Damascus. He had won his race. Lawrence and his men had accomplished the seemingly impossible. No one could ever take this historical fact away from him.

October 1, 1918 should have been the greatest day of Lawrence's life. He was following in the footsteps of conquerors whose glory has not died, even in the modern world—the Babylonian Nebuchadnezzar, the Persian Cyrus, the Greek Alexander the Great, and the Roman Pompey. His name was about to be added to the ages. He was to take Damascus, the pearl of the Arab world, symbol of past Arab power and strength, and he was to do so at the age of 30. At this fateful moment, literally nothing seemed beyond him.

The night before, unable to sleep, Lawrence could see the sky over Damascus white with flame, as the German troops that were seconded to the Turkish army blew up the ammunition dumps in the city, before the entire Ottoman-led army fled. Fearing that the entire city would be put to the torch, Lawrence dropped off into fitful slumber. However, he awoke, to see "instead of ruins, the silent gardens stood blurred green with river mist, in whose setting shimmered the city, beautiful as ever, like a pearl in the morning sun."[9] The city was his for the taking.

Damascus had been the Holy Grail of the Arab Revolt. It was the thread running through everything Feisal and Lawrence had done for the past two years, since their first fateful conversation in Hamra. Spurred on by a combination of Feisal's inherent political legitimacy and ability to keep the squabbling tribes together and Lawrence's imagination, Damascus was for them what Jerusalem had been for the Crusaders. The ultimate Arab goal was to turn success in the war into the stable basis for an independent, self-governing Arab state, with, "foundations large and native enough to employ the enthusiasm and self-sacrifice of the rebellion, translated into terms of peace."[10] Lawrence hoped to capitalize on the emotional high point of capturing the city to catapult the Arab state in Greater Syria into being.

On the fateful day Lawrence was to enter an open Damascus with the Ottoman troops in flight, and achieve his triumph, he stopped to wash and shave in a little stream on the outskirts of the city. He was there set upon by an Indian sergeant from Sir Henry Chauvel's nearby Australian forces, who thought he had captured a fleeing Turkish prisoner and promptly if briefly arrested him. As Lawrence was wearing full Arab dress from head-to-toe, it was an understandable mistake. However his arrest threw off Lawrence's timetable. The Australians under

Chauvel entered the outskirts of Damascus at 6:00 A.M. on October 1, the Arab army the city's center at 7:30 A.M., and Lawrence, following his detention, at 9:00 A.M.

And what an entrance it was. Riding in Blue Mist, the hero of the Arab Revolt drove down the main avenue of the city, which was packed with nearly a quarter million people lining the sidewalks, standing on balconies, and craning their necks out of windows. They chanted the names of Arab heroes, first "Feisal," then "Urens," which is the exact Arab transliteration of "Lawrence." At town hall, the scene was even more exuberant. A mob was there, yelling, embracing, dancing, and singing. Lawrence, overcome with emotion, cried like a baby with thankfulness.

Lawrence had arrived just in time. Chauvel finally made it to the center of the city by 9:30 A.M., only 30 minutes after Lawrence arrived at the town hall. Despite Allenby's orders that the Arabs alone were to take the city, on September 30 Chauvel's Australians had marched through the center of Damascus, heading for the suburbs on the north side of the city where they had been ordered to deploy, inadvertently if fleetingly "liberating" it. The next morning Chauvel decided to have a look at things in Damascus proper.

Meeting him, Lawrence irritatingly assured Chauvel that he, and he alone, was responsible for public order, until the arrival of Allenby and Feisal. Further, he lied, saying that his candidate for civil governor, Shukri Ayubi, had already been "elected" by the townspeople. Chauvel's Australians were welcome to enter the city center the next day, but should stay away from Damascus until then, as the greatest celebration in centuries was likely to occur that night.

Dubious, but in the face of a *fait accompli* and with firm orders from Allenby not to enter the city unless forced to, Chauvel reluctantly agreed. While Lawrence had not exactly been first to Damascus, he had bluffed his way to the prize. He now had a slender window to establish Arab administration in the city without British or French interference.

But Lawrence had another problem. Within the Arab population of the city, there were opportunists hoping to take advantage of the chaos in Damascus to rule in Feisal's name. Two Algerian brothers, Mohammed Said and Abd el Kadr, had raised the Hashemite flag in Damascus on September 30, as the Turks and Germans fled the city. They had been supporters of Ottoman rule until literally the day before, but now they saw an opportunity to seize local control. Said, with the tepid backing of Feisal's ill cousin Nasir, proclaimed himself the civil governor of Damascus.

Lawrence had several very good reasons to hate the disreputable pair. Both were openly pro-French, with a very ambiguous record of supporting Feisal, as they had played the Turks and the Arab army off one another for their own political benefit. Lawrence felt certain that el Kadr was the turncoat who had alerted the Turks to one of his most ambitious guerrilla raids, an effort to dynamite the Yarmuk Bridge, dooming the adventure to failure.

Perhaps most chillingly, Lawrence believed that Said had been the very man to personally denounce him to the Turkish garrison at Dera, where he later said he was repeatedly raped and brutalized earlier in the war, in November 1917.[11] To stare directly into the face of the man who, whatever happened at Dera, he certainly regarded as an implacable cause of so much of his own personal emotional suffering on this of all days wades deep into historical irony.

Sending for the Algerians, Lawrence was told by their servants they were sleeping. Dryly, he suggested that they be awakened. As the brothers approached Lawrence in the town hall, he surrounded himself with the Rwalla tribe, his own personal bodyguard, and the Arab army regulars under his friend, Nuri Said, the future prime minister of Iraq, who Lawrence had appointed commander of Arab troops in Damascus. Lawrence was taking no chances with this slippery pair.

Lawrence abolished their one-day-old government and told the Algerians that he was installing Shukri as governor of the town. A snarling Mohammed Said denounced Lawrence as a Christian and an Englishman, and urged his old friend Nasir to stand by him.

Nasir, embarrassed, said nothing. Then Nuri Shalaan, chief of the Rwalla tribe, stepped into the fray. Quietly declaring that Lawrence had his people's personal support, Nuri's intervention politically doomed el Kadr's hopes. Abd el Kadr played the only card he had left, assassination. He lunged at Lawrence with a dagger, only to be confronted by Auda, who pummeled el Kadr until he was subdued. At this decisive moment Lawrence's Arab friends had stood by him. Still, it is striking that immediately upon joining that list of immortals who have conquered Damascus, Lawrence was set upon by a knife-wielding assassin. Treachery was in the air.

Nor were the brothers quite finished. Lawrence was awoken from his first night's sleep in the capital with the alarming news that Said and el Kadr were stirring mutiny among the Damascenes by suggesting that Lawrence's actions had been nothing more than a British ploy to seize the city for themselves. They managed to recruit a good number of Arab Druse, a tribe that had not risen for Feisal but lived in the city and around it, to their cause. As dawn broke on the morning of October 2, the Druse were looting shops on the city's outer limits. Nuri Said, whose men were camped in Damascus itself, aimed his machine guns at the mob, crushing the nascent quasi-rebellion.

The storm passed as quickly as it had arisen; by midday the Druse had been disarmed and normalcy had returned to the city. El Kadr managed to flee, though his brother was captured and imprisoned. But there soon was a reckoning. Just one month later, in November 1918, el Kadr was shot dead by Arab police, supposedly trying to escape as they came to arrest him. But the charge that el Kadr had leveled, that the British might have ulterior motives in Damascus, was rather too close to the mark.

Meanwhile, in terms of actually governing the city, there was so much to do, and all at once. Lawrence set out to restore a degree of control through Shukri, until Feisal and Allenby arrived. Damascus was in chaos, as Lawrence's wartime comrades began looting, killing some Turkish prisoners in cold blood. From the moment he found himself helping administer Damascus, Lawrence tried to stop the rampage and eventually succeeded in lessening the chaos.

During that first day, October 1, Lawrence and Feisal's new government tried to: organize a police force; clear the water supply of the rotting carcasses of dead men and animals; secure an engineer to keep the power generators working; set up a sanitation commission; organize a fire brigade; take over the city's prisons; organize relief work by opening Turkish warehouses to distribute food to the starving; establish a newspaper; replace the currency; repair the railway so that food could enter the city. For the first time in two years, the streets were hosed down of their perpetual dust.

There can be little doubt that Lawrence's initial efforts met more than their fair share of success. Within days, British servicemen began to roam the city as sightseers, rather than as occupying forces. Later, the self-sustaining nature of the Arab government in Greater Syria was a powerful argument in favor of asserting that the Hashemites indeed had legitimacy there.

But at the time a worn-out Lawrence could see only the Arab tendency to chaos, and the British proclivity for Great Power duplicity. He makes clear in *Seven Pillars of Wisdom* that at the end of that first day he was thoroughly disillusioned. Visiting a pestilential makeshift Turkish hospital that had been sacked by Arab looters, Lawrence's existential doubts continued to grow. For there, amid the stench and the rot, with standing pools of blood and the dead and dying being gnawed on by rats, he found seven Turkish doctors, rather than trying to put right this deplorable state of affairs, instead sipping tea and making toffee. Appalled, Lawrence ordered them to attend to the wounded. When they were slow to respond, he ordered his aide, Lieutenant Kirkbride, to draw his revolver. It finally sent them scurrying to do their duty.

On the following day, Lawrence revisited the hospital, hoping to see that conditions had improved. A British major in the Medical Corps, just entering the city that day, happened upon the hospital and saw the fly-covered squalor. Taking him for an Arab, he asked Lawrence if he was in charge. He replied that yes, he supposed he was, in a way. To which the Major bellowed, "Scandalous, disgraceful, outrageous, you ought to be shot."[12] Imagining what the officer might have said had he been present the previous day, Lawrence cackled with laughter, losing what was left of his self-control. Outraged, the major yelled at Lawrence, "Bloody brute!" and slapped him across the face before stalking off in a fury.[13] It was an inauspicious end to what had been a glorious military campaign. But far worse was yet to come.

The miracle of Arab unity was only the first stage of Lawrence's dream. The second vital step was gaining international recognition for Arab independence. As always, it came down to the attitude of the British. Feisal wryly remarked on the Arab dependence on its enigmatic ally. "We are delighted to be your friends, most grateful for what you have given us, but do, please, remember that we are not British subjects. We should feel more at ease if you were not so disproportionate an ally."[14]

On October 3, 1918, Allenby and Feisal finally arrived in Damascus. The prince had ridden into the capital at a gallop to a tumultuous welcome. Feisal and Allenby met, with Lawrence acting as interpreter. For the first time in two years, he was in the physical presence of both of his masters, who personified his hopes that the interests of the Arabs and the British would prove complimentary.

But Allenby had come bearing bad news. The French, not fooled by the race to Damascus, were demanding their promised gains in Syria and Lebanon. Allenby announced to a disbelieving Feisal and Lawrence that Syria would be a French protectorate. Feisal was to have the administration of the Syrian interior, minus Palestine and Lebanon, under French guidance, with Paris directly controlling the Syrian coastal ports. France would immediately send a liaison officer to act as advisor to Feisal, alongside Lawrence. In other words, Britain was insisting on the enforcement of the Sykes-Picot Treaty, after repeatedly lying to Feisal about its importance.

It was not Britain's finest hour.

Strenuously objecting, Feisal insisted that he would accept neither French guidance nor a French liaison officer; he meant to be completely independent. He refused to recognize France's authority over Lebanon, and demanded control of at least one Syrian port, so that the new Arab state would be economically independent. Feisal also caustically noted that Lawrence—Allenby's own liaison officer—had promised him all of Greater Syria, excluding Palestine. He was prepared to accept British assistance, believing that as his advisor Lawrence would work with, and not try to dominate, local elites.

Allenby wanted to know if what Feisal said was true. In a state of exhausted shock, Lawrence confirmed Feisal's account: He had not told the Prince that Syria was to be a French protectorate. Strictly speaking, the answer was accurate. But the two men had talked at length about Sykes-Picot, though they had both firmly believed that winning the race to Damascus would trump the French claim, a point of view the British had encouraged.

His insight, expressed years earlier in a letter to his parents, that, "So far as Syria is concerned it is France and not Turkey that is the enemy,"[15] had been proven true at the critical moment in Damascus. His illusions had at last been shattered. Taking the city had been a military triumph for him, but amounted to a personal and political tragedy.

Allenby, summoning up all his martial authority, reminded Feisal that he was a serving lieutenant general in the British forces under his command and therefore must accept French domination of Greater Syria, at least until the coming peace conference. Feisal, deeply disillusioned, melted away. The meeting, which dashed all of Lawrence's hopes and dreams, had lasted a mere 15 minutes. The principle that had underwritten all of Lawrence's efforts in Arabia, that British and Arab interests were indistinguishable, had proven to be false at the critical moment in Damascus.

After Feisal left, Lawrence stayed behind to talk to Allenby. Lawrence quietly told the British commander that he would not serve with a French liaison officer under Feisal. He reminded Allenby that the army owed him leave, and said that he would like to take it immediately. "Yes, I think you had,"[16] Allenby retorted. Lawrence had just one request: he wanted to be promoted to colonel so that he could travel back to Britain with a first-class rail ticket and have his own berth on the ship home. Allenby promoted him on the spot. An Arab diplomat to whom Lawrence described this pivotal moment, later recalled that the reason for Lawrence's dramatic decision to flee the field of treachery had been a simple one: "if there was no alternative to applying the agreement [Sykes-Picot], there remains no place for him in Syria."[17]

The Arab Revolt had furthered the British strategic goal of dividing and weakening the Ottoman Empire, but, in the end, Britain's need to maintain France as a close ally was more important to them than keeping their promises to Lawrence and Feisal. The guilt Lawrence felt was tremendous. In a letter to the *Times* of London published nearly a year afterward, the editors suppressed a paragraph in which Lawrence admits that he told the Arabs that the postwar settlement would not forget them and that he bitterly regrets his "perjury." His personal reputation made his word unchallenged among Arabs. Lawrence's realized that he had been the perfect tool of British *realpolitik*.

So the conqueror of Damascus came to realize that his primary role in the war had not been as a facilitator of the Arab Revolt, but as a political pawn, who could keep the Arabs in harness, while the British weighed the competing claims of Feisal and the French. European duplicity had brought the Arab movement to a dramatic halt at the moment of its greatest triumph.

Chapter 5

"The old men came out again and took from us our victory, and remade it in the likeness of the former world they knew."

—Lawrence on the postwar settlement
Seven Pillars of Wisdom

As for so many peoples, the Paris Peace Conference of 1919–20 proved the final undoing of Arab hopes, laying the groundwork for future instabilities and further conflicts. Faced with the problem of dividing the spoils of the Ottoman Empire in the Middle East, the British government found itself in a moral and diplomatic dilemma. In the case of Greater Syria, both France and the Hashemites had been assured of British support as the war ran its course. The opulent palace of Versailles was the place where these conflicting bills came due.

Ten days before the opening of the peace conference designed to put an end to the possibility of all future wars, Lawrence accompanied Feisal to Paris. Due to French pressure, the emir attended the conclave not as a representative of Greater Syria, but as a delegate representing the Hejaz of his father. The Hejazi delegation stayed at 72 Avenue Bois de Boulogne, while Lawrence bunked down at the Continental Hotel with the rest of the British delegation. Again, Lawrence served two masters. He had been made a technical advisor to the British delegation and was also representing Arab interests. Lawrence's role in the service of Feisal was more all-encompassing. He was the emir's diplomatic confidant, inseparable companion, finance minister (he managed the British Foreign Office grant, which kept the Arab delegation afloat) and translator. This unusual bureaucratic arrangement affirmed Lawrence's continuing hope that British and Arab interests, even following the treachery of Damascus, were ultimately one and the same.

Lawrence's central goal in the negotiations was to free Feisal from French domination. The Arabs wanted an independent Syria run with British assistance. Lawrence had set out the basic Arab position in a memo he wrote to the British Cabinet's Eastern Committee on November 4, 1918. He began by citing Hashemite loyalty to the allies throughout the war, neglecting to mention the numerous incidents of hesitation and flirtation with the Turks, and then set forth his major proposal, and that Feisal be made king of Greater Syria. Lawrence argued that Feisal must have the freedom to appoint his own foreign advisors: "Feisal requires to be sovereign in his dominions, with complete liberty to choose any foreign advisers he wants of any nationality he pleases. These advisers will be part of the Arab government and will draw their executive authority from it and not from their own government."[1]

He further proposed that three new Hashemite kingdoms be established in the Arab world, with Feisal's brothers, Abdullah and Zaid, ruling Lower and Upper Iraq respectively. He wanted to create the Shia province around Basra for Abdullah and the Sunni province around Baghdad for Zaid. Within the British foreign policy bureaucracy, Lawrence's initiative was supported by the War and Foreign Offices and roundly criticized by the paternalistic India Office.

Feisal had the support of the Syrian people, evidenced by the self-sustaining government he continued to run from Damascus. Looking back, Lawrence made this critical point about Feisal's legitimacy in Syria, writing in *Seven Pillars,* "Our aim was a façade rather than a fitted building. It was run up so furiously well that when I left Damascus in October the fourth [1918] the Syrians had their de facto Government, which endured for two years, without foreign advice, in an occupied country wasted by war, and against the will of important elements of the allies."[2] The Arab government proved a hardy weed indeed.

A Syrian observer described Feisal's first return from the peace conference to Damascus in the spring of 1919, "When His Highness Emir Feisal arrived at Damascus, he rode in a carriage drawn by eight horses. The carriage was trimmed with gold and silver. Victory arches had been set up for him and were decorated with jewels donated by the women of Damascus. Spread before him in his path were 25,000 carpets."[3]

But harnessing the enthusiasm of the Syrian populace proved a double-edged sword for Feisal. He was open to compromise and, if it had been left to him alone, he may well have been able to work out a deal with his erstwhile allies, Britain and France. But the Syrian people, while wholly behind the prince, wanted their expectations from the war, whetted by British promises, to be at last met. If there was no doubting Feisal's legitimacy in Syria, what its people wanted was equally clear; full independence. Even among his personal staff in Damascus, many of them

Mesopotamian army officers who had led the revolt, nationalist feeling was strong and unbending.

Thus, swept along by local passions and aspirations, Feisal did not have the political wiggle-room to make compromises at Versailles. This tension in the Arab negotiating position remained a problem throughout the conference. An account of Feisal's second trip back to Damascus from Versailles during the time of the conference paints a different picture, one of almost unbearable political pressure on the Emir. Feisal "met well-wishers who had organized a great demonstration in which 120,000 participated, demanding unity and complete independence. His Highness announced that he was fully committed to unity and that he would accept nothing but complete independence."[4]

Looking back from our own jaded age, it is hard to recapture the enthusiasm Woodrow Wilson inspired following the end of the Great War. The twenty-eighth president, a stern man of unbending superiority, was also an eloquent speaker, who had mesmerized his audiences with the dream that a better world was theirs for the taking. By drawing on the enormity of the human pain and sacrifices made in the course of the war, Wilson proclaimed that the only thing that could give such suffering meaning was a transformational peace, without the usual grubby territorial annexations.

Wilson's idealism was like a ray of sunshine, puncturing the gloom of a world still shocked by four years of barbarism. For many, Wilson's idealism cast a peculiarly similar glow to that of today's veneration for Barack Obama; it was the first genuine ray of hope in memory. He inspired huge crowds across Europe as he made his way to the palace of the later Bourbon kings. However, dangerously for the president, Prime Minister David Lloyd George of Britain and Premier Georges Clemenceau of France felt exactly the opposite way; only significant territorial acquisitions could begin to compensate the two countries for all that they had lost. From this fundamental difference, the Versailles Peace was to emerge, making a mockery of Wilson's grandiose dreams.

In terms of practical statecraft, the lofty American president proved no match for his more earth-bound interlocutors. Wilson's "Fourteen Points," his beguiling outline of a program for a new world order based on international law and self-determination among nations which served as the basis for the American negotiating position in Paris, was hopelessly vague in practical policy terms. Worse, Wilson had at the same time unrealistically raised the world's expectations of the coming of a glorious new age to the point that any real-world agreement would inevitably seem shabby in comparison. This doomed the treaty in terms of public relations, as no agreement, and certainly not one as unenlightened as Versailles, could make the horror seem worth it. Clemenceau got the spirit of the thing right. Commenting on the Wilson's "Fourteen Points," he cruelly observed, "Fourteen points: that's a bit much. The good lord has only ten."[5]

Regarding the lands of the former Ottoman Empire, Wilson proclaimed in Point Twelve of the "Fourteen Points" that the peoples liberated from by its demise should have the right of "absolutely unmolested opportunity for autonomous development."[6] This unambiguous language would seem to wholly favor Feisal's negotiating position over that of the imperialistic French. However, in truth, settling the Arab claims was merely an afterthought for statesmen who had to redraw the map of Europe and try to put into practice Wilson's grand vision.

By the time decisions began to be made about the future of the Middle East, Wilson was already in severe domestic political trouble. The Democratic president had arrogantly and foolishly refused to include any senior Republicans in the American delegation to Versailles. As such, the opposition party had no stake at all in supporting a treaty which it had no part in creating. Wilson was rigidly unprepared to make the slightest compromise to the resurgent Republicans in Congress. America's involvement in Europe was to be a casualty of Wilson's stubbornness, with isolationism becoming the dominant American foreign policy of the immediate post-Wilson era. Wilson's clout in Paris decreased in direct proportion to the rise of his domestic political problems. The president was to see only four of his cherished "Fourteen Points" fully implemented.

Despite recent efforts by some historians to resurrect the reputations of the peacemakers of 1919, there can be little doubt, based on the empirical evidence, that Versailles was one of the supreme failures of modern diplomacy. Historian David Fromkin is surely right to say "Nothing, however, could have provided a better description of what was going to happen at the Peace Conference than Wilson's speeches about what was not going to happen. Peoples and provinces were indeed 'bartered about from sovereignty to sovereignty as if they were chattels or pawns in a game.'"[7] For the Arabs, American help—so beautifully expressed in Wilson's eloquent, if empty, rhetoric—was to prove another false dawn.

$\mathcal{T}he$ French, on the other hand, were nothing if not consistent. The leader of their delegation, Prime Minister Georges Clemenceau, was the living embodiment of French nationalism and resistance. He had hated many things in his life, but above all, Germany. In 1871, a young Clemenceau had been a member of the French National Assembly that had strenuously protested Germany's harsh peace terms at the close of the Franco-Prussian War, which had seen France cede to Berlin its cherished provinces of Alsace and Lorraine. Now, as the last survivor of that doomed gathering, Clemenceau had the delicious opportunity for revenge that he had been awaiting throughout most of his adult life.

Clemenceau had never been popular with his parliamentary colleagues, having made a name for himself by exposing their many corrupt practices. However, he inspired fear in his enemies, equally as a biting speaker and proficient duelist. In France's darkest hour in 1917, with the French army in open mutiny and with the country in despair, at last his colleagues turned to him as prime minister. Reestablishing a sense of purpose in both the French army and the French nation, constantly visiting the front lines and rallying his people, Clemenceau never wavered in his belief in the country's ultimate total victory. He became known as *Le Pere de la Victoire,* the father of victory.

Like Wilson, he came to the Paris Peace Conference at the height of his reputation. Also like the vainglorious president, domestic woes were to severely hinder his freedom of maneuver at Versailles.

Seventy-nine years old at the start of the conference, Clemenceau had by then grown both deaf and fat. However, in late February 1919, he still managed to live up to his nickname, "the Tiger." He was shot in the chest by an anarchist would-be assassin but somehow managed to return to the conference by the beginning of March. Clemenceau quickly grew frustrated with both the lofty Wilson and the slippery

Lloyd George, shouting at them both in a most undiplomatic manner as the peace talks progressed.

Clemenceau's position at Versailles was simple; Germany must never be allowed to harm France again. It is hard now, following the ghastly twentieth century, to convey what a shock the devastation of World War I was at the time for Western civilization. It has been estimated that the combined total of military and civilian casualties in all Europe's wars in the hundred years between 1815 and 1915 was not greater than a single day's combat losses in any of the great battles that took place from 1916 onward. Although he employed very different tactics from Wilson, Clemenceau surprisingly shared the same ultimate goal: such a bloodbath must never be allowed to happen again.

The premier believed that the key to the French position remained Britain. During an earlier term as prime minister, in 1906, Clemenceau had helped cement the *Entente Cordiale,* which underwrote the subsequent Anglo-French wartime alliance. As such, he was an avowed anti-colonialist, prepared to defer to the British on these issues in order to secure unwavering British support against Germany. On the face of it, this general diplomatic strategy would have seemed to suit both Lawrence and Feisal, as it would allow for a revision of the hated Sykes-Picot Agreement.

On December 1, 1918, Clemenceau met privately with Lloyd George at No. 10 Downing Street. In line with his overall strategy, the Tiger offered the prime minister the province of Mosul, today's northern Iraq, which had previously been guaranteed to Paris under Sykes-Picot. In addition, Clemenceau said that he would raise no objection to Britain's controlling Palestine. In return for avoiding colonial controversies with his primary ally, the French premier expected British support for France's other colonial demands. Above all, this meant French dominance of Greater Syria.

Despite his personal anti-colonialism, Clemenceau, like Wilson, had powerful enemies. French public opinion was strongly for the annexation of Greater Syria. Having suffered two million casualties in the war, the French people wanted some tangible return for this ghastly sacrifice. In addition, the powerful Catholic lobby wished to extend the Church's missionary work in Syria, while nationalists and colonialists alike underlined France's historical roots in the region, supposedly dating back to the crusades. These powerful forces constantly provided a check on Clemenceau's anti-colonialist sentiments. As the conference progressed, officials in the French Foreign Ministry organized a campaign to further inflame French opinion against their own prime minister. In *Le Temps* and *Le Journal des Didots,* they accused him of ceding too much to Lloyd George.

This domestic constraint was a constant tension in Clemenceau's negotiating position that forced him to remain resolute in upholding the terms of Sykes-Picot regarding Greater Syria. Lawrence had entirely underestimated both the French determination to colonize Syria and Lebanon and the role colonialism then played in sustaining French national pride.

In the negotiations, the British, as ever, clung to a middle view, which placed them between the vague but potent American idealism of Wilson and the cold fury of French desires for revenge against Germany. At the end of the conference, when asked how it went, Lloyd George replied, "Not badly, considering I was seated between Jesus Christ and Napoleon."[8]

Lloyd George wanted to punish Germany, but, unlike Clemenceau, he did not wish to destroy it. A key figure in British liberal governments for a decade, Lloyd George, like Clemenceau, came to power when the war was at low ebb for the Entente. Like the French premier, he was credited with reviving his country, and after the war, as was the case for all three primary figures at Versailles, his reputation stood at its zenith. A brilliant double-dealer, the Welsh Wizard was strong on tactics, if short on overall grand vision, proving himself the polar opposite of the American president.

Going into the conference, the British government, advised by Lawrence, hoped that the Americans would pressure Clemenceau into giving up his claim to Syria so that the Sykes-Picot Agreement could be declared dead. The British knew they were in a bind. On October 29, 1918, Lawrence had appeared before the Eastern Committee of the War Cabinet in London. Lord Curzon, the acting foreign secretary, effusively praised the newly minted war hero. Following this tribute, Lawrence ungraciously, if accurately, burst out, "Let's get to business. You people don't understand the hole you have put us all into,"[9] causing the emotional Curzon to burst into tears. From this point on, he was to become a bureaucratic enemy of Lawrence.

In spite of this, things started promisingly enough for Lawrence. He had visited the Foreign Office the day before, on October 28, 1918, to discuss Arab matters with Sir Robert Cecil, the aristocratic assistant secretary for foreign affairs. Cecil privately showed him a draft of an Anglo-French proclamation, which seemed to be the definitive word on doing away with Sykes-Picot.

Part of the reason for this seeming change in course was that both the British and French governments feared the worldwide admiration (bordering on hysteria) for President Wilson and his "Fourteen Points." They felt compelled to treat the latter, at least rhetorically, as the morally just basis for a global peace. Signed on November 7, 1918, the Anglo-French Declaration was a way to deal with popular opinion in their own countries, while giving them time for gauging at the peace conference if Wilson actually meant what he said. Lawrence was again caught between Franco-British rhetoric and Franco-British *realpolitik*.

Nor was Lawrence the only major figure pressing the British government for changes to Sykes-Picot. No less an expert than Sir Mark Sykes, author of the document in question, declared to the Eastern Committee of the War Cabinet, "The Agreement of 1916 was dead, although the French refused to admit it. What was required now was some modification of, or substitute for, that Agreement."[10]

With even Sykes (who was soon to die in the Great Spanish Influenza Epidemic) disowning his own handiwork, the British government adopted a promising negotiating strategy for Versailles, from the Arab perspective. On December 18, 1918 the Eastern Committee reached agreement on Britain's Middle Eastern strategy for the conference. Regarding Syria, it was decided, "to back Feisal and the Arabs as far as we can, up to the point of not alienating the French."[11]

While on the surface this sounds like a clear diplomatic victory for the Arab cause, in reality the language reflected the tension inherent in the British negotiating position. While the initiative was certainly an effort to square the circle of having made too many promises to too many allies, in reality Lloyd George had at last made a choice.

Despite all the high-sounding words and soothing promises, the British government, especially with American influence fading, was primarily interested in maintaining its intimate ties with France. And of course Lloyd George was interested in furthering his own imperial objectives in the Middle East. Only as an afterthought did what the British owed to Feisal and his Arabs come into play. Ultimately, Feisal's cause was a very low-ranking goal for London, one that would be easily traded away to secure primary British interests.

Lawrence, who created a sensation by wearing Arab dress on the streets of Paris, was there to participate in the diplomatic minuet first-hand. Though he initially enjoyed his growing notoriety, as time passed he grew increasingly frustrated with the slow pace of decision-making at Versailles—where the Middle East negotiations took a back seat to the discussions regarding the future of Germany and a sustainable European peace—and increasingly suspicious of the motives of the great Western powers. However, socially, Lawrence did little to help Feisal's cause. In fact, in one disastrous act of schoolboy rage, the conqueror of Aqaba threw toilet paper down several flights of stairs at British Foreign Minister Balfour.

On February 6, 1919, the Arab case for self-determination was made before the "Big Four," who dominated conference decisions: Prime Minister Lloyd George of Britain; Prime Minister Orlando of Italy; Premier Clemenceau of France; and President Wilson of the United States. Lawrence, wearing an Arab headdress, made the address, with Feisal and Nuri Said also in attendance.

Speaking in English and French, Lawrence laid out the Hashemite position: the Arabs had been steadfast allies during the war, and Feisal should be king of Syria with complete freedom to choose his foreign advisors. It was over this last point that the entire drama hinged. For if it was agreed that Feisal was free to choose advisors, Sykes-Picot was no longer in force. It would then be up to local Arabs, rather than to Great Powers thousands of miles away, to determine the destiny of Syria.

Following his great disillusionment in Damascus, Lawrence finally had reason to believe that he could secure Feisal his throne and his wartime comrades their due. He hoped that President Wilson, who had made himself the global champion of local self-determination, through Point Twelve of the "Fourteen Points," would commit himself to Syrian independence.

Allenby's army was still deployed in country, and Lloyd George announced that it would not withdraw until a decision had been made about the political future of Greater Syria. Allenby thus gave the British practical leverage over the French as they were de facto the western force on the ground, which meant the French could not simply march into Damascus and impose their will. Also, with British troops on the front lines, London wanted stability in Syria above all to safeguard their army, a state of being that could only be guaranteed by Feisal's fledgling government. Local British and Arab interests looked to be intertwined; Lawrence placed his hopes on these facts on the ground eventually translating into diplomatic realities in Versailles.

Wily Premier Georges Clemenceau, the survivor of decades of French politics, had other plans. Throughout the conference, he and French Foreign Minister Aristide Briand urged private bilateral discussions with Feisal to reach an agreement; despite what Wilson had preached, secret diplomacy had not yet outlived its usefulness. Clemenceau, with the nationalistic French press shrilly behind him, demanded that Sykes-Picot be carried out as the only possible basis for a Middle East settlement.

Playing for time, Lloyd George compromised. On March 25, 1919, Britain, France, and the United States agreed to send a commission to Syria to investigate local opinion, especially regarding which Great Power should be the region's protector. The commission was led by Henry King, the president of the prestigious American university Oberlin College, and Charles Crane, a Chicago businessman and major donor to Wilson's Democratic Party. This was broadly in line with both Wilson's and Lawrence's principles.

Feisal, believing that the outcome could only be in favor of Britain or America, both of whom would exercise considerably less direct control than the notoriously imperialistic French government, saw this as his greatest victory. For the first time in his life, Feisal drank alcohol— champagne—in celebration of escaping the clutches of the French.

France, fearing the King-Crane commission so welcomed by Feisal, went to him with a compromise deal. On April 13, 1919, with the King-Crane commission on its way to Damascus, Clemenceau met privately with Feisal and Lawrence, to try to reach a political agreement between France and the Hashemites. There are several different accounts of the meeting, but it appears the French and the emir neared a compromise. If Feisal accepted the French mandate and its control over Syrian foreign affairs, he would be crowned king and Syria would have its domestic independence from Paris. In many ways, this was the very deal that Lawrence and his comrades had hoped for from the British, or at worst case, the Americans.

Some accounts of this meeting have Lawrence seeing this as a major step forward and, fearing that the conference was already failing to live up to its utopian promises, urging the prince to accept. Others say that he told Feisal to reject the offer, believing that the French, given their notorious top-down colonial record, were simply not to be trusted. French and Arab accounts further diverge; the Hashemites said that they refused the French overture, while Clemenceau and the French press claimed that Feisal agreed privately to the deal at first, then went back on his word. Whatever the truth of the matter, the French and Feisal ultimately failed to come to terms.

Finally, in August 1919, the King-Crane commission did return a verdict in favor of an American protectorate for Greater Syria. However, by then their decision was unimportant, as in the interim it had become apparent that isolationist winds in America were imperiling the Wilsonian dream. Britain and France, left to come to agreement regarding the Middle East on their own, simply ignored the commission's report. Lawrence's friend and ally Gertrude Bell, present at the conference as an expert for the British government on the Middle East in general and Mesopotamia in particular, denounced the King-Crane affair as a criminal deception. For while the British had paid lip service to the aspirations of the Syrian people, in reality they were to be left to the tender mercies of the imperialist powers. After this incident, it became clear to Feisal that there was no escaping the French.

While the King-Crane commission was investigating, Lawrence and Feisal had temporarily gone their separate ways. Feisal returned to Damascus for the first time since the conference opened, April 16, 1919, having achieved little in his four months in Paris. In an effort to shore up his legitimacy in the eyes of the Western powers and to influence

King-Crane, he called a Syrian General Congress for June 6, 1919. It was summoned to endorse the prince's negotiating position at Versailles, by showing him to be the authentic spokesman of the Syrian peoples. While dominated by his army officers, there is little doubt that Feisal's position, calling for genuine Syrian independence under his rule, was met with genuine local enthusiasm.

While Feisal was tending his base, Lawrence was wearing his other hat, that of British imperial adventurer. He suddenly and mysteriously left Paris on May 3, 1919. London had called on him to put out another fire in the Middle East. The Arabian potentate, Ibn Saud, at the head of the puritanical Wahabi religious revival that had energized and inspired primarily eastern Arabian tribes through its religious fervor, was challenging the balance of power in the Arabian desert. He threatened Hussein's stronghold in Mecca, while simultaneously attempting to crush the third major political power in the region, the tribes around Ibn Rashid.

Allenby was taking no chances. He ordered Lawrence to take charge of the Hashemite defenses around Mecca in anticipation of a Wahabi onslaught. In the end Ibn Saud, fearful that the 60,000 pounds a year he received from the British exchequer was in peril, withdrew for the moment, settling for the obliteration of Ibn Rashid, which increased his power in the Arabian peninsula as a whole. But this incident was the first tangible sign that the Hashemite position in Arabia, on which Lawrence based so much of his strategic thinking, might not be as stable as it seemed.

On his way to the Near East to bolster the Hashemites in the face of the Wahabist onslaught, Lawrence almost lost his life in a plane crash in Rome. While both the pilot and copilot of his plane were killed, the hero of the desert war again cheated death, escaping with a broken collarbone and fractured ribs. Taking his time after the Ibn Saud threat receded, Lawrence convalesced in the British Embassy in Rome and then went on to Cairo to visit the Allenbys, where his boss had been installed as the new British high commissioner. He returned to Paris, July 7, 1919.

Awaiting him in Paris was the most fascinating woman of the age, his old friend Gertrude Bell. In her slightly outdated Edwardian dresses—complete with frilly hats, piercing high-pitched voice, and demanding manner—she at first seemed to emerge as some sort of caricature of the pre-war era. However, she was not to be underestimated.

The first woman to receive a first-class degree from Oxford, she had been an early Alpinist, climbing the Matterhorn in 1904. Scholar, archaeologist, traveler, adventurer, Bell was the most famous author of books about the Middle East before the war. In her travels alone throughout Arabia, her knowledge of the tribal structure of the region, and her determination to play a central role in policy-making in what was very much a man's world, Bell showed herself to be a preeminent Middle East expert as well as an effective bureaucratic infighter.

Born into a family of great wealth, Bell had been encouraged to excel in all fields, a rarity for Edwardian women. Using her family's extensive connections to the full, she had great influence with the bureaucratic powers-that-be in London.

Bell had come to Versailles a firm believer in the necessity of direct British top-down rule throughout its colonies. In Paris, she renewed her earlier brief association with Lawrence, who she had met as a scruffy apprentice archeologist at Carchemish before the war. After spending most of the Versailles conference in the charming company of Lawrence and Feisal, Bell's views had changed 180 degrees.

Lawrence shrewdly noted the reason for her conversion. Speaking of his friend years later, he caustically said, "she was not a good judge of men or situations: and was always the slave of some momentary power: at one time Hogarth, at another Wilson, at another me, and last Sir Percy Cox. She changed her direction each time like a weathercock."[12]

But there were other reasons for Bell's change of attitude. She had seen Arabs governing themselves in Feisal's name in Syria. She had witnessed the fervor of Arab nationalism in both Palestine and Syria. Facts on the ground, plus the charismatic pleadings of her friends, had pushed her to declare that British power and influence could best be served by the more indirect approach of devolution.

Like Lawrence, for all her accomplishments, Bell remained an outsider, both because of her gender as well as her somewhat off-putting, Eleanor Roosevelt–like manner. She was the era's true bluestocking. Passionate and often unhappy, Bell was cursed by a series of unfulfilling love affairs with doomed men. As was true of Lawrence, ignoring the traumas of her private life only seemed to increase her fervor to do right in the public sphere. This fascinating pair proved to be Feisal's greatest allies.

The solution to the British dilemma was never really in doubt. Though many in the government, including Prime Minister Lloyd George, had sympathy for both Lawrence and the Arab cause, London had never been likely to side with Prince Feisal. When the prime minister saw that Wilson would no longer be available as a reliable ally, and that America was likely to withdraw from a prominent role in international politics, he was thrown back into the arms of Clemenceau. Feisal was tossed overboard, as Britain reversed its mildly anti-French Middle Eastern policy.

France, as Britain's primary World War I ally and a needed bulwark against a defeated but vengeful Germany, was always a more important British interest. The Sykes-Picot Agreement won out over the assurances the British had made to Emir Hussein and Prince Feisal during the war and its immediate aftermath. In the end, the British betrayed the promises they had made to Lawrence, and through him, to their Arab allies.

Worse still, both Britain and France intended to rule their new subject peoples as though the Great War, and the desire for local self-determination that it encouraged, had never happened. Centralized, direct control from far-away London and Paris was to remain the norm in the Middle East. This unimaginative and always disastrous political formula has been followed in the modern era by the United States in Iraq and elsewhere, with predictably ruinous results. Lawrence's new stakeholder approach was brushed aside, as old-style *realpolitik* won out.

Lawrence and Feisal failed in Versailles for three basic reasons. They underestimated French military power and Paris's determination to control Syria. The Great War had bled France white, and Clemenceau was under extreme pressure, be the outcome anti-Wilsonian or not, to take the maximum number of geopolitical prizes he could.

Then, they had been wrong about the British, who, with their foreign policy loyalties divided and with France the more important ally, were never going to come to Feisal's rescue in 1919–1920, even if it was the morally correct thing to do.

Lastly, the United States unexpectedly turned away from Wilson's foggy dreams, revealing America's lack of interest in the Middle East settlement, which it increasingly left to Britain and France. Lawrence and Feisal were betrayed by French opposition, British calculation, and American apathy.

Seeing the outcome as now determined, the British establishment moved against Lawrence, ahead of Feisal's return to London in September 1919, following his second trip back to Damascus. He was excluded from all further negotiations. The government was rightly concerned about his loyalty, given that he was clearly out of step with Lloyd George's revised Middle East policy. Lawrence did not join Feisal as he left London for Paris that fall. From the Autumn of 1919 until the start of 1921, when Winston Churchill invited him to join the Colonial Office's new Middle Eastern Department, Lawrence had no part in making British government policy. Many in the establishment hoped that he would grow discouraged and simply fade away.

At the same time, Lloyd George and his cabinet, in bilateral meetings with Feisal in London on September 19 and September 23, 1919, told him that Britain had no further interest in Syria, and that all British troops would be withdrawn from the country by November 1. Washing their hands of their Arab allies, the British cabinet had the nerve to advise Feisal to attain the best terms he could get from Clemenceau; they would play no further role in mediating between Paris and Damascus.

Having little choice, Feisal accepted the advice of the British cabinet and again met privately with Clemenceau. In January 1920, they arrived at a compact. Nominally Syria would be independent, but Feisal would have French advisers. Clemenceau promised a loose mandate over Feisal's government, but given France's standard imperial pattern of top-down rule, this was unlikely to occur in reality. Clemenceau had essentially offered Feisal the Sykes-Picot terms: he was to be made the ceremonial king, while France actually ruled Greater Syria as a client state. Feisal, with his back to the wall, accepted.

But this agreement proved too much for both the French and Arab elites, so far apart were they on the future direction of Syria. Clemenceau insisted that the talks must remain strictly secret, as he was then running for president of France, and worried any concessions he made to Feisal would jeopardize his chances with the nationalistic French public.

Clemenceau was right to worry; he was defeated for the presidency and resigned as premier on January 17, 1920. With his defeat, the provisional agreement was never ratified by either side. It is a sign of the times and of French feeling that the Tiger was destroyed for being perceived as too accommodating to all parties: Germany, Britain, and the Arabs. His successor, Alexandre Millerand, did not accept the deal with Feisal, nor did he wish to make any further arrangements with the Hashemites. At last the mask was off; the French intended to rule Syria entirely as they pleased, regardless of local public opinion.

But the French were not the only people in the thrall of nationalist fervor. When Feisal returned to Syria on January 14, 1920, he was accused by nationalists of selling out the Arab cause to Clemenceau. Realizing that he could easily be swept away by the passions roused by Versailles, Feisal repudiated the recently made agreement, and shortly thereafter the Syrian General Assembly followed suit, voting down the Feisal-Clemenceau concord.

The die was cast. On March 7, 1920, the Syrian National Conference, a quasi-parliament dominated by his former staff officers, proclaimed Feisal king of Greater Syria, and declared itself to be completely independent from all vestiges of foreign control. Feisal, grasping hold of the nationalist tiger and knowing that personal survival meant that he could not afford to let it go, accepted the Conference's wishes.

Only a month after the Arabs had proclaimed Feisal king, in April 1920, the Treaty of San Remo was signed by the major powers in Italy. It was a far cry from the Wilsonian promise that had so captivated the world. The San Remo conference was an offshoot of the Versailles conference that was designed to tidy up the Middle Eastern settlement. The treaty awarded France and Britain mandates that challenged Feisal's hold on his new kingdom. Rather than merely recognizing French and British interests and spheres of influence in the Middle East as Feisal and the Arabs had hoped, the San Remo Treaty actually awarded Arab territorial control directly to Western powers, in line with the standard practice of nineteenth-century imperialism.

The terms of the Franco-British deal at the April conference in Italy were later confirmed by the Supreme Allied Council, the body of nations that was to ratify all side agreements that were part of the Versailles process, in the Treaty of Sevres on August 10, 1920. While the Sykes-Picot agreement, with its noxious reputation, was never ratified, the portions of it that were the most injurious to the Arabs were included in the San Remo and Sevres pacts.

In essence, the treaty divided up Greater Syria into modern Syria, Lebanon, and Palestine, with the French acquiring the two former countries and the British gaining the latter, Transjordan (today's Jordan), plus modern-day Iraq. Gone was any pretense to a Wilsonian settlement based on the Lawrencian principle of local self-determination and local autonomy; San Remo and Sevres amounted to nothing less than the standard European power grab. If one were looking for a root cause for present Arab anger at the west, it would be well to look in detail at what happened following the Great War.

This volatile situation was made worse as Feisal, under immense pressure from his officers, allowed his followers to carry out guerrilla attacks against French personnel and property on the coast of Syria. This was all the pretext the French needed. Using these attacks as a cause for battle, the French army, under the command of General Henri Gouraud, invaded Syria in July 1920.

France was not about to lose what it had so arduously won at the negotiating table. On Bastille Day, July 14, 1920, Gouraud sent an ultimatum to Feisal that he believed would never be accepted: he demanded that the Arab army disband. Feisal, well aware of what modern weapons and troops could do to his comrades in pitched battle, remarkably agreed to the terms.

This was too much for the people of Damascus. They rioted against the emir, taking to the streets, accusing him of "selling the nation like merchandise,"[13] and denouncing him as a traitor. Insurgents attacked the palace, and a gun battle broke out between Feisal's Royal Guard and the nationalist rioters. The people of Damascus had surely been behind Feisal throughout the Versailles process; but as proved true for leaders in the United States, Italy, and France, they were more for their own conception of nationalism, than they were supportive of any specific leader. Feisal had equivocated with the French, so his domestic standing was put in peril.

However, Feisal's unexpected concession was not enough for Gouraud, itching as he was for a fight. He sent a message to the emir, incredibly stating that his offer to disband the army was unacceptable. In desperation, and despite the previous Arab nationalist reaction, Feisal offered Gouraud his unconditional surrender. Gouraud disingenuously replied that the message had come too late. The French began their march on Damascus.

On July 24, 1920 the two armies met at the town of Maysalun, 12 miles west of Damascus. While Feisal had ordered his Arab army not to resist, Yusuf al-Azmeh, his defense minister, insisted on putting up a defense. The Arab fighters numbered about 3,000, but only a few hundred regulars were amongst their ranks. The rest of the army consisted of hastily summoned citizen-volunteers from the city.

The French, on the other hand, numbered 9,000 disciplined colonial troops, largely from the French African colony of Senegal. The French, equipped with machine guns, tanks, and airplanes, panicked the Arab troops with the tools of modern war. Gouraud also brutally gassed the Arabs, who quickly disintegrated as a fighting force. The battle was over almost before it began; 42 French soldiers had died; Arab losses amounted to almost ten times as much, at 400 killed. Among the dead was the young defense minister, al-Amzeh, just 36 years old.

The war had lasted a mere five days, and on the July 26, the French marched into Damascus. On the 28th, Feisal was taken by the French to a railway station in the city and left to take a train into exile in Italy, and then London. Lawrence and Feisals' dream of real Arab independence for his wartime comrades had ended in Western duplicity and Arab tragedy. After reaching Damascus, Gouraud put his stamp on the whole unsavory business. Walking to Saladin's grave, Gouraud is supposed to have kicked it, shouting at the Arab hero of the Crusades, "Awake Saladin, we have returned! My presence here consecrates the victory of the Cross over the Crescent."[14] Whether such sentiments formed a solid basis for rule in the twentieth century is not a question that seems to have bothered the darling of French colonialism.

In keeping with its standard top-down approach to colonial governance, the French quickly substituted their language for Arabic in Syria's law courts. Meanwhile, Millerand proclaimed that Syria would be ruled by France, "The whole of it, and forever."[15] At last the French had shown their true diplomatic colors. Feisal and Lawrence had been right to fear them during the long months in Versailles.

But almost as soon as the disreputable settlement was put in place, cracks began to appear. The close Franco-British ties, welded together by the fire of the Great War, were never quite the same in the interwar era. Nor would the Arabs ever again wholly believe glib British promises. In trying to be all things to all men, the British had ended up being distrusted by both the Arabs and the French alike. Such is the practical diplomatic price to be paid for longstanding duplicity.

On the face of it, Britain and France had been entirely strategically successful. Through lies, deceit, and power politics, they had managed to turn the energies of Lawrence, Feisal, and the Arab Revolt into a tool for substituting their rule in the Middle East for that of the defeated

Ottomans. But by ignoring the lessons Lawrence had learned and by disdaining local political opinion in Syria and the Arab world, which Lawrence rightly saw was central to effective governance, the Western imperial powers doomed themselves to running perpetually unstable and unsustainable colonies. Not for the last time would a top-down external approach lead to failure in the Middle East.

Tragically, more had been lost in Syria than just a Hashemite throne. Without doubt Feisal had possessed genuine political legitimacy in Damascus; the great hope of building a stable Arab government in the region had been decisively dashed, due to Great Power politics. Given all that has happened since then in this most tumultuous region in the world, the West would come to bitterly regret unseating Feisal.

According to his mother, no longer able to help his friend, Lawrence had watched from his family's home in Oxford the unfolding tragedy in agony, staring straight ahead for days, eating little and talking less. It seemed that everything he had fought for, everything he believed in, had come to nothing. Here he was truly representative of his "lost generation," having been deprived of the fruits of a better world after suffering so mightily for the old one. But he was not yet finished. The next months would bring about a startling reversal of fortune, reunite Lawrence with Feisal, and give him a last chance to make things right for his Arab comrades.

Just after the war, Lawrence had written to Geoffrey Dawson, the influential editor of the *Times*. Pressing the Arab cause, Lawrence noted, "They never had a press agent, or tried to make themselves out a case, but fought as hard as they could . . . and did it without, I believe, any other very strong motive than a desire to see the Arabs free."[16] He would now be that press agent. He would now be that advocate. For one other important thing had occurred as Lawrence had endured the numbing duplicity of Versailles.

He was now arguably the most famous man in the world.

Chapter 6

"Suddenly I awoke to find myself famous."

—Lord Byron, 1812, on his becoming a global celebrity,
following the publication of *Childe Harold's Pilgrimmage*

At the end of World War I, the British public knew little about the Arab Revolt and even less about Lawrence. The British elite was the first to discover him. Lawrence arrived back in England a genuine war hero in a conflict that had been more characterized by the squalor of the trenches than by glamour. He was a full Colonel, who had received battlefield advancement due to his heroism. Allenby had recommended Lawrence for a knighthood. The British upper class was quick to claim such a man as one of its own.

Upon returning to Britain in October 1918, at the urging of the Arab Bureau, the British Cabinet's Eastern Committee put Lawrence to use as an Arab expert, immediately soliciting his opinion about what should be the postwar settlement in the Middle East. He began canvassing politicians and newspaper owners and editors, especially Geoffrey Dawson of the *Times* on the unjust plight of the Arabs. In three *Times* articles that appeared between November 26 and 28, 1918, he portrayed the Arab Revolt a sort of romantic crusade, with a Hollywood-like account of Feisal as a modern-day King Arthur. It was blatant propaganda, introducing a largely ignorant British public to the revolt in the desert, a tale told entirely from Lawrence's perspective. Single-handedly, he kept the Arab cause in the news.

At the turn of the century, it was the dream of almost every English schoolboy to be presented with a decoration for gallantry by the king-emperor. On November 30, 1918, Lawrence was in a position to live out this childhood fantasy. In a private ceremony at Buckingham Palace, he was to be officially awarded his Companion of the Bath and also given the Distinguished Service Order, two of the highest awards for gallantry it was possible to win in the British Empire. King George V himself would present the awards, which was a conspicuous honor, and there were rumors that one more token of esteem was to come. The Victoria Cross, the highest award for gallantry in the Empire, might well have been his, or the knighthood that many of his senior colleagues in the Arab Bureau would come to receive. We will never know for certain, for, at the ceremony, Lawrence, in front of the monarch himself, refused both decorations.

Things had started well enough. Lawrence presented George V with his personal firearm, a .303 rifle, as a gift. It had a curious history, having been taken from the British during the fighting at Gallipoli, the scene of one of the Empire's worst defeats in World War I. Symbolically, it was given to the Turkish leader, Enver Pasha, as a token of the Ottoman Empire's greatest victory, who covered it with gold chrome. As part of an inducement to keep him loyal to Constantinople, Enver had in turn given it to Feisal, who, not very long after, bestowed it upon Lawrence, as a token of Anglo-Arab friendship (it now resides in the Imperial War Museum in London). In giving it to the king, Lawrence was making the broad point that friendship among men and between peoples should be honored.

But it was his quiet but stirring words on this occasion that shook London society. Lawrence told the king that he could not honorably accept such decorations because of the British government's refusal to keep faith with the Arabs. George V's private secretary, Lord Stamfordham, later wrote of the king's recollection of the occasion. "In asking permission to decline the proffered decorations, Colonel Lawrence explained in a few words that he had made certain promises to King Feisal: that these promises had not been fulfilled, and consequently, it was quite possible that he might find himself fighting against British Forces, in which case it would obviously be wrong to be wearing British decorations."[1]

This was Lawrence's declaration of war against the British establishment that had so turned against him in Damascus. He had finally made a choice: he intended to put personal honor above loyalty to his country. Lawrence had pledged his word to Feisal and now the British government was about to let the Arabs down by siding with the French over Sykes-Picot. Lawrence told the king that he was a leader of sorts among the Arabs and that he intended to stick with his friends through thick and thin, if necessary fighting the French to safeguard Syria for them. He hoped the king would forgive any want of courtesy that he had shown. The king later remarked that he "had been left holding the box"[2] full of his country's highest decorations.

Lawrence's version of events was similar. He later told his friend and bureaucratic ally Winston Churchill that refusing the honors was the only way he felt he could rouse the highest authority in the land to realize the great wrong Britain had done to Feisal and the Arabs. Lawrence sincerely felt the honor of his country was at stake because of its double-dealing and betrayal of the Arab cause. Churchill, however, felt strongly that he had been wrong to create such a scene; Lawrence replied that the king should be aware of what was being done in his name.

Despite the fact that this was a major breach of royal protocol, the king at the time seemed taken aback, but not offended. Like so many others, he was intrigued by Lawrence. Socially, Lawrence had taken a grave risk, as his actions could well have spelled his doom among the very British elite that he needed to win over if he was to get justice for Feisal and the Arabs.

However, the gamble paid off. One of the social maxims governing the British Edwardian upper-class world revolved around the strict necessity to always tell the truth and to keep one's word; another was the imperative to remain loyal to one's friends. In begging off personal glory for these very English reasons, Lawrence became a *cause célèbre* among the British upper class, as much for upholding these very English virtues as for his sterling military record. Whether consciously or not, Lawrence had once again used local cultural knowledge, this time of his own people, to further his ends. Word soon spread of his actions, which were, on the whole, judged to be brave and manly. The incident came to be seen as a wonderful story of honor. Lawrence's fame began to grow.

The ultimate sign that the British upper class had forgiven him came when George V invited Lawrence, this time with Feisal, back to the palace on December 12, 1918. Lawrence appeared, to the shock of the courtiers, in full Arab dress alongside the emir, yet another symbolic statement of the ties that bound the Anglo-Arab cause. Lawrence had, quite brilliantly, brought Feisal's plight to the attention of the very people who could alter his fate. His battle with the British establishment had begun.

But it was a stage production known as "The Last Crusade: With Allenby in Palestine and Lawrence in Arabia," which catapulted him to stardom. During the spring of 1917, the American journalist and entrepreneur Lowell Thomas had approached John Buchan, the great British novelist and then director of the British Department of Information, looking for a story to stir up pro-British sentiment in the United States. Buchan eventually directed Thomas toward the Middle East, where Allenby was soon to capture Jerusalem at the end of the year.

In early 1918, Thomas caught up with Allenby in the ancient capital and met Lawrence, who happened to be back at headquarters, reporting on the Arabs progress in the desert. Thomas knew immediately that he was on to something, but he could not begin to realize what this chance meeting would mean for both their fortunes.

Intrigued, Thomas briefly joined Lawrence back in Arabia, in the Spring of 1918, where he shot film and made slides of the Middle Eastern campaign, but the war ended before they could be put to propaganda use in the United States. Undaunted, Thomas creatively turned his material into a live theatrical event. He would lecture about the Arab campaign for two hours, while film and hand-colored slides, complete with musical interludes, flooded the stage; for its time it was a very professional and high-tech production.[3] In March 1919, Thomas launched his extravaganza at the Century Theatre in New York.

In this age of mass media, it is almost impossible to truly understand the effect the program had on an audience that had never heard or seen a talking movie. To a public sickened by the war in the western trenches, Thomas's focus on the Middle East, and especially the desert campaign, seemed exotic and full of adventure, with bonafide heroes, none more heroic than Lawrence. Thomas called it, "the most romantic story of the war."[4] Though he had spent only a few weeks in the spring of 1918 with Lawrence, Thomas confidently called him "the uncrowned King of Arabia"; never mind that the production was wildly historically inaccurate. Astride his war camel, charging out of the wastes of the Arabian Desert, exuding mystery, courage, and chivalry, allied to a brave colonial people fighting for their freedom, Lawrence allowed the American people forget the charnel house of the Western Front.

On August 14, 1919, following a successful run in New York, Thomas brought his show to London, where it was an immediate critical and commercial success. In the service of entertaining the public, Thomas, who was only 27 years old at the time, simplified the story of the revolt in the desert to the point that the audience likely imagined that Lawrence and his camel had triumphed alone in the wastes of Arabia, so completely did he dominate Thomas's show. In a few short weeks, by the end of the summer of 1919, Lawrence was a national hero.

But far more adulation was to come. Thomas moved the show from Covent Garden to the larger Royal Albert Hall, where it was booked for a six-month run. It quickly became the most popular production of its day, with an estimated one million Britons taking it in. The king himself asked for a private showing. In 1920, at the Queen's Hall, Thomas gave a Royal Command Performance.

There was no doubting that Lawrence was the star of the extravaganza. The short section of the film on Lawrence, which had originally been merely an interlude in a show that focused on Allenby in Palestine, was consistently rated the highlight of the program. Determined to give the public what it wanted, Thomas changed the name and the focus of the show from "With Allenby in Palestine" to "The Last Crusade: With Allenby in Palestine and with Lawrence in Arabia," highlighting the exploits of the warrior-scholar, the youthful conqueror of Damascus, Colonel Thomas Edward Lawrence, late of the British Arab Bureau.

The sight of the matinee-idol-looking Lawrence in full Arab dress, charging through the desert on a camel with his heroic, underdog Arab army, was a far more popular diversion for the British general public than Allenby's Palestinian adventures. Seizing on the production's fame, Thomas went on a world tour, traveling to the United States twice, Canada, Britain, Australia, New Zealand, Southeast Asia, and British India. It was a triumph wherever it went. An estimated four million people, including a self-mesmerized Lawrence, saw the show around the world. In the words of Lord Byron, Lawrence "awoke to find himself famous." He was the world's first modern celebrity, a war hero-matinee idol combined; his life would never be the same.

As for the star himself, despite his almost constant grumbling to his wartime comrades about the show's inaccuracies, Lawrence, from the beginning, was both obsessed and repelled by Thomas and the fame that the show brought him. After attending its first night at Covent Garden, Lawrence left a note for Thomas, saying, "Saw the show last night and thank God the lights were out."[5] Yet Lawrence went to see it at least five times, reportedly thrilled and disgusted in equal measure. Also, secretly, he helped Thomas with his often-inaccurate book, *With Lawrence in Arabia,* published in 1924, which became a transatlantic bestseller as a follow-up to the production. Thomas went on to become one of America's best-known radio presenters for decades to come. The Lawrence hoopla had made his career.

The Thomas book was just the beginning. As the twenties progressed, Lawrence became something of a cottage industry; every artistic endeavor associated with his name seemed to turn to gold. Lawrence's own abridged account of his experiences, *Revolt in the Desert,* a forerunner to *Seven Pillars,* was published in 1927, to both glowing reviews and worldwide commercial success.

The well-known writer Robert Graves published a biography of Lawrence, *Lawrence and the Arabs.* Also released in 1927, it, too, became a bestseller. In 1934, Basil Liddell Hart, the noted historian and a friend of Lawrence's, produced a second biography of him, *T. E. Lawrence: In Arabia and After,* that was also commercially successful. This constant rehashing of the Lawrence tale turned him into the rarest of creatures: a man who was national history in his own time, part flesh and blood, part imperial myth.

L awrence would use his astronomical fame to further his political cause. Through a prolific (if not always wholly accurate) letter-writing campaign to British newspapers, Lawrence cultivated British public opinion in an effort to reestablish the link between the fortunes of Feisal's family and British interests.

In the May 30, 1920 *Sunday Times,* he wrote that the British at-tempts to deceive Feisal had been wrong, saying, in a classic bit of British understatement that must have played well with his readers, "It was not for such politics I fought."[6] The statement could stand as a general epi-taph for the whole sorry Treaty of Versailles. Tapping into the growing disillusionment of his whole generation with the results of the confer-ence, Lawrence tried to make the debt of honor he personally felt Britain owed to Feisal and the Arabs a matter of national conscience.

In two articles in the *Daily Express* of May 28–29, Lawrence had taken a more statesmanlike tone, criticizing London for not reacting to the major strategic changes occurring in Asia and acting instead as though the Great War had not altered anything. He argued that the problem with British colonial policy in the Middle East was bureau-cratic, stemming from the fact that the region was the responsibility of three separate British cabinet departments—the Foreign Office, the India Office, and the War Office—beset by internal rivalries, who often pursued their own policies independently of the others, rendering over-all British foreign policy in the region schizophrenic.

If Lawrence was quick to take advantage of his fame; he also, in his passive-aggressive way, was not above promoting it. Many observers of his career, then and now, have rightly commented on the two sides of his character. Lowell Thomas, who had shrewdly perceived both the Lawrence who was above it all and Lawrence the showman, famously said that he had a genius for "backing into the limelight."[7] Sir Harold Nicolson, senior Foreign Office grandee and diarist, noted Lawrence's role in creating his own myth, saying, "he discovered early that mystery was news."[8] Basil Liddell Hart felt that Lawrence was responsible for a good deal of the mythmaking around him, noting Lawrence was like "a woman who wears a veil while exposing the bosom."[9] Indeed many people came to see him as a charlatan, more the creator of his own fame, perpetuated through his very public efforts to denigrate it, rather than someone who had actually done anything noteworthy.

The assessment was unfair. Perhaps Sir Robert Vansittart, Lawrence's second cousin on his father's side and a pillar of the British establishment, made the definitive character sketch of Lawrence. He was a not always sympathetic observer of the fame swirling around the "uncrowned king of Arabia." But Vansittart was certainly just in simply saying that Lawrence "was a show-off with something to show."[10]

While Lawrence at times certainly did encourage the perpetuation of his myth, solid achievement continued to lie beneath it. Throughout the 1920s, he labored on his masterpiece, *Seven Pillars of Wisdom,* his impressionistic account of the Arab Revolt. In various draft forms it received the highest praise from the lions of British literature: Thomas Hardy, H. G. Wells, and Rudyard Kipling.

No less a writer than George Bernard Shaw, who with his wife Charlotte became a sort of surrogate family for Lawrence at this time, called him, "one of the greatest descriptive writers in English literature."[11] Though the book was only published after Lawrence's death in 1935, it has never since been out of print, a fact which would certainly gratify him, as he valued writers and artists beyond all men.

Written in the Homeric style befitting an Oxford graduate, *Seven Pillars of Wisdom* is the only modern epic. Yet it is also a surprising military history. In telling the story of the Arab army's revolt against the Turks, Lawrence added a personal, psychological dimension that was entirely lacking in the great Greek and feudal dramas he so admired. It is the dichotomy between the vast—a story encompassing World War I and Lawrence's progress through the endless wastes of the desert—and the miniature—interior battles raging within one man—that gives the work its unique quality. It remains a masterpiece of modern literature.

Yet Lawrence, much as he yearned for artistic success, continued to feel unworthy to compare himself to the other great writers of his day. Certainly, in the story of the Arab Revolt, he had magnificent material to work with, and he told the story well. But he had been uniquely placed to do this; following it up was to prove difficult. His next and last book, *The Mint,* published many years after his death, recounts Lawrence's later life as an anonymous serviceman. It has its moments, but lacks the verve and scope of its predecessor. Lawrence was never quite certain he belonged to the literary pantheon he so admired.

It is safe to say that Lawrence's celebrity gave him the contradictory feelings of pleasure and torment, almost from the beginning. Yet it could not be undone. As early as 1919, the press was already calling him, "the most interesting Briton alive."[12] Lawrence used his celebrity soapbox to make himself an indispensable member of the British foreign policy commentariat. By 1920, he was viewed by the wider public as the preeminent British authority on the Middle East. Lawrence was to turn the power of public opinion into genuine bureaucratic heft.

It is undeniable that Lawrence parlayed his fame, especially after Maysalun, into bureaucratic success in helping make things right with Feisal. His celebrity, as much as anything else, paved the way for him to personally and dramatically change British policy in the Middle East. He could never have taken on the establishment and won without it.

One thing more helped him; he had been proven right. By the end of June 1920, not for the last time, Iraq was on fire.

Chapter 7

"There is a dry wind blowing through the East, and the parched grasses await the spark."

—John Buchan, *Greenmantle*

Feisal and his men had not been the only Arabs to feel duped by the peace process—the Anglo-Arab declaration of November 1918 had seemed to promise to the Arab elites in Baghdad as well that self-government was on its way. They, like Feisal, were to be disappointed.

In December 1918, feeling both local pressure for home rule as well as the international cry for self-determination encouraged by President Wilson, the Eastern Committee of the Foreign Office instructed Arnold Wilson, the acting British ruler of Mesopotamia, to sound out local opinion on its desire to have an Arab ruler. Wilson shamelessly rigged the process by talking primarily to those who agreed with him during winter of 1918–1919, receiving the result which best suited his views. In early 1919 he concluded that, while the Arabs in Mesopotamia favored an Arab ruler, they were nowhere near a consensus as to who it might be. On this point, Wilson may have been factually accurate. But it was certainly a stretch to conclude from this that the vast majority of Arab elites pined for a continuation of the British occupation. At best, Wilson was deluding himself into hearing what he wanted to hear. At worst, his behavior was an egregious example of top-down British imperialism.

Wilson had other plans for Iraq. Only 36 years old in 1920, he seemed to belong to the earlier Victorian era, both in terms of his personality and his politics. He was tall, handsome, arrogant and unapproachable, stoical to the point of being taciturn. He despised all activities he viewed as frivolities, hating dancing, gossip, and idleness in equal measure. Beyond all this, this last Victorian believed most fervently in the direct British rule of the late nineteenth century.

At the time, newspaper pundits nicknamed Wilson, "The Despot of Mess-Pot," given his autocratic style; he thought subordinates and local Mesopotamians were best when seen and not heard. He was not used to and did not accept criticism of his judgment, even from London. In short, he was the sort of man Lawrence innately despised.

Wilson governed Mesopotamia from April 1918 until October 1920. He was a characteristic representative of the India Office, which had been given the lead role in administering Mesopotamia following British victory over the Turks. The bureaucratic ethos of the India Office in general and of Wilson in particular advocated a colonial policy of direct British rule.

The India Office, believing in one-size-fits-all thinking, sought to model governance in Baghdad on Britain's imperial rule in India. The British government in Iraq had reversed the prewar system of relying on Arab officials, instead feeling that the Arabs were unfit for such responsibility, and in need of coming generations of colonial rule before being allowed even a taste of self-government. Instead, the India Office severely restricted the number of official positions open to Iraqis. In 1917, there had been only 59 British officials serving in Iraq's civil administration. By 1920, under Wilson's leadership, this number had swelled to 1,022. Arabs held less than 4 percent of jobs in the senior grades of their own country.[1] This program ran against all culturally accepted political norms. Not only were the British not living up to the high-sounding promises of independence that they had proclaimed in the war's latter stages, they also were actually taking away Arab power by centralizing what had been left to the locals for generations. This refusal to work in harness with local elites, a Lawrence maxim, helped fuel the 1920 revolt.

Whatever the Foreign Office in London had in mind, Wilson was not about to budge from his conviction that Mesopotamians needed to be saved from themselves. He wanted nothing less than to transform Iraq into an outright colony, directly ruled by the British administrator in Baghdad. Regarding Iraq, Lawrence came to see Wilson and the India Office as his implacable philosophical foes.

Such a centralized top-down approach flew in the face of the Mesopotamian cultural experience. Iraqis were bound to resent Britain imposing centralized rule over an area that had grown used to the Ottoman Empire's largely decentralized style over the past four hundred years. The Mesopotamians, living far from Constantinople, were used to a good deal of de facto autonomy, especially as Ottoman power waned. Wilson, flying in the face of both historical and cultural realities, set the spark that was to ignite the insurrection.

Wilson was also determined to include Kurdistan into what was soon to be known as Iraq, uniting the three Ottoman *sanjaks,* or governing regions, of Mosul, Basra, and Baghdad, into one country. Before

1920, Iraq had never been a country, nor the Iraqis a people, for good reason. The ruling Ottomans had gotten it about right, dividing the area into three provinces that corresponded to the local unit of politics, which was based on ethno-religious divisions: Basra, dominated by the Shia Arabs; Baghdad, dominated by the Sunni Arabs; and Mosul, dominated by the Kurds

History, culture, religion, and geography pulled these three groups apart, not together. As late as June 1918, no railway linked Basra in the south and Baghdad in the center of this fledgling country together; the two regions were entirely isolated from one another. Basra looked toward its natural allies and co-religionists, the Shia, in Persia, today's Iran. The Sunni searched for like-minded allies throughout an Arab world dominated by their view of Islam, while the Kurds favored their kinsman in Turkey and Syria. These ethnic, tribal, and religious groupings trumped any thought of national cohesion. The Kurds were restless at the thought of Arab domination, while the Shia resented the power of their Sunni Arab brethren. In other words, Iraq then looked a great deal like it does today. The British should have known better than to think such an artificial political entity could produce stability.

Moreover, Wilson wanted to make these drastic changes on the cheap. Britain, in an effort to economize following its breakneck spending during the Great War, undermanned its garrisons throughout its expanding Empire, even as many Arabs under British occupation felt a temptation to right the many wrongs that had been done to them. The Treaty of San Remo had given credence to the Arab world's worst fears; far from winning their independence as had been promised, they were to merely have a new master: London instead of Constantinople. This final act of diplomatic treachery crystallized anti-British feeling throughout the region. The reckoning for British duplicity had come.

On June 30, 1920, just a month after Britain was awarded the mandate in Mesopotamia, a largely spontaneous rebellion exploded, spurred on by London's effort to collect local taxes. However, the underlying cause of the revolt was the result of the dashed hopes for self-determination that Woodrow Wilson had inspired. Not for the last time, the liberators in Iraq quickly became seen as oppressors.

By the summer of 1920 one-third of the country, especially in the Kurdish north and the Shia-dominated south, was in open revolt. At first, the insurrectionists had the upper hand, with the surprised and undermanned British garrisons being put on the defensive. By mid-August, the insurrectionists felt strong enough to proclaim a provisional Arab government throughout the region. Things turned so bleak that the British were forced to summon reinforcements from India to combat the rebels.

The tide eventually turned for the British, but at a gut-wrenching cost. Reacting harshly to the rebels' challenge to its authority, Britain sent punitive military expeditions to burn villages in the countryside while the Royal Air Force (RAF) bombed Iraqi rebels from the air, acts that horrified the British public. By February of 1921 the rebellion finally subsided, but at the cost of 2,000 casualties and 450 British lives; well over 10,000 Iraqis, many of whom were civilians, were also killed.

Beyond these gruesome numbers, the rising was a financial disaster for a Britain that could ill afford it. Suppressing the Mesopotamians cost the British exchequer 40 million pounds, two times Iraq's annual budget, and three times the total in subsidies that Britain had paid to Feisal during the entire the Arab Revolt.

Predictably, Arnold Wilson followed what would become a depressing pattern for failed nation-builders throughout the twentieth century: the inevitable call for more resources. Seeing Mesopotamia as a military problem, Wilson urged London to strengthen the British military presence in the country as a way to head off future uprisings. His deputy, the inimitable Gertrude Bell, strenuously disagreed, and began working at cross-purposes with her boss. Now, post–Paris Peace Conference, squarely in the Lawrence camp, she instead urged her many friends in London to install an Arab-led government in Mesopotamia as a way to establish future stability in the war-torn country. The die was cast for a larger debate about the future direction of the British Empire.

In a memo written to the Foreign Office on September 15, 1919, just before he had been relieved of his duties for the peace conference, Lawrence had predicted that a continuation of British top-down imperial policies would lead to a major outbreak of violence in the Middle East by around March 1920; he had been off by just a matter of months. Within the establishment, Lawrence received great credit for being right; it enhanced his expert status and won him a large number of supporters within the British government.

But the revolt did more than simply elevate Lawrence's status; it also severely discredited both Wilson and the India Office.[2] For Lawrence, in a series of newspaper articles, made sure the public knew all about the horrible mistakes that had been made by the British in Mesopotamia before the revolt.

Beyond this, Lawrence was also gathering support from influential friends in the army, the civil service, and the House of Commons to aid his cause. An all-party group of MPs was established to take a fresh look at the Middle East, under the leadership of Conservative MP Lord Robert Cecil; Lawrence's old friend, Tory MP Aubrey Herbert; and the Labour MP, Colonel Josiah Clement Wedgwood, who had also served in the Middle East during the war.

This all-party group provided Lawrence with significant political and bureaucratic support. On July 15, 1920, just after the Iraqi crisis had begun, Herbert asked the embattled government whether Iraq could be returned to the pre-war system where the Arabs had largely been in charge, and had cost the British government only 3 million pounds a year. The push for decentralization in the name of economy was to be a major plank of Lawrence's ongoing campaign to change the nature of British imperial policy. Because by the summer of 1920 Iraq represented more than a stray difficulty; the British Empire as a whole was mired in a severe general crisis, a new political reality that, more than anything else, allowed Lawrence, at last, to best his foes just one year later.

In what was historically a blink of an eye, the British Empire had descended from its post-Versailles high-water mark into a desperate crisis for survival. The British were suffering from a classic case of "imperial overstretch," whereby their global commitments far outran their ability to shape events. Historically, such a syndrome has been the disease that has destroyed great powers from the Roman Empire to Napoleon's

France. The British were to prove no exception to this geopolitical rule. Simply put, Britain had bitten off more than it could chew.

Despite its victory in the Great War, the British Empire faced a systemic crisis. From 1919 onward, the government was increasingly alarmed that its imperial commitments were leading to disaster. The bad news came from all corners of the globe. Britain was supporting the reactionary white revolutionaries in their doomed fight against the Bolsheviks in Russia, and had garrisons in Germany, Constantinople, Syria, Iraq, and Persia. The Third Afghan War had flared up. There was an anti-British uprising under Saad Zaghul Pasha and the Wafd Party in Egypt, which was only suppressed with great violence as British troops fired on rioting nationalist crowds, while the RAF, as during the Mesopotamian revolt, bombed civilians. A Kurdish rebellion north of Mesopotamia was suppressed by Arnold Wilson and British soldiers. The 1920 insurrection in Mesopotamia proper took 40,000 troops to put down.

The British also had to suppress insurgency in the Punjab, which led to the infamous Amritsar massacre, and the rise of the Congress Party led by Mahatma Gandhi. General Reginald Dyer's massacre of hundreds of Indian nationalists at Amritsar in northwestern India was a scandal that had morally discredited the whole imperial system, causing ordinary Britons to have second thoughts about their country's massive commitments around the globe. Ireland continued to fester, as it had done for decades. Kemal Attaturk, rallying Turkish nationalism, succeeded in pushing Western troops out of Anatolia, where Britain, France, and Greece had attempted to impose their will on the core remnant of the Ottoman Empire. In terms of both finances and manpower, the British Empire found itself in great peril. Everything the Empire, so recently at its apogee, touched seemed to turn to lead.

These serious setbacks were compounded by a severe British economic slump. In 1920 the British economy went into a pronounced recession. Exports declined, prices sagged, and the country was gripped by mass unemployment for the first time in the modern era. In such an environment, it is no wonder that both politicians and the general public alike began to question whether Britain could afford to dabble in far-flung foreign policy adventures in places like Palestine and Mesopotamia.

Nor did the British have the military flexibility to deal with these multiple global crises. After the Great War, there was an understandable desire in all quarters for demobilization to proceed as quickly as possible, whatever the geopolitical consequences. In June 1919, a few weeks before Lawrence's visit to Egypt, there had been a series of mutinies by British troops, protesting the slow pace of returning the mass armies needed in the Great War to civilian status. In 1920, Sir Henry Wilson, the chief of the Imperial General Staff, submitted a memo to the cabinet, warning that Britain had no reserves to reinforce its hard-pressed garrisons around the world should the need arise.

With the economy in a free-fall and British military commitments straining London to the breaking point, Britain needed a whole new modus operandi to salvage its Empire. This played directly into Lawrence's hands. The mood of the country toward imperialism was shifting, both on practical as well as philosophical grounds. In an August 7, 1920 editorial, written at the height of the Iraqi insurrection, the *Times* asked "how much longer are valuable lives to be sacrificed in the vain endeavor to impose upon the Arab population an elaborate and expensive administration which they never asked for and do not want?"[3]

The Mesopotamian insurrection became the key immediate foreign policy reality aiding Lawrence's campaign. The cabinet's sensible response to intense geopolitical and domestic pressure was cost cutting and a corresponding decrease in global commitments, in line with the new general mood of the country for retrenchment. It was in this environment of crisis and limits that Lawrence intensified his newspaper crusade, which gained momentum in a context of imperial peril. In countless newspaper articles, the hero of the desert pressed the fiscal point. This, plus the national conscience, led the British establishment, so recently his sworn enemy, to come cap in hand to Lawrence to help sort out the mess.

Lawrence, writing three newspaper articles in the summer of 1920, with the insurrection in full swing, sought to undermine British imperial policy in the public mind, replacing it with his stakeholder-driven approach. In a letter to the editor that was published in the bastion of British conservatism, the *Times,* on July 22, he linked Britain's dire financial situation to the need for an overall change in colonial policy, advocating more local control as a cost-effective way to save the Empire. In the left-wing *Observer* of August 8, he wrote a piece which reserved special scorn for the India Office and Arnold Wilson. Wilson and his minions were directly in the way, both politically, and, more importantly, intellectually, of everything that Lawrence stood for. Lastly, in the *Sunday Times* of August 22, he linked the British debacle in Iraq to the recent French takeover of Feisal's kingdom in Syria, rousing liberal imperialists by noting the brutal similarities between the two colonial powers.

What was most important about the articles, other than their exquisite timing, was that Lawrence did more than criticize; he positively and clearly promoted a policy alternative to old-style colonial rule for saving the Empire. Also, he stayed on message, using a series of repetitive themes in the pieces to drive his point home with the broader public. No less an authority than his archenemy Arnold Wilson interpreted the government's looming change of policy towards Iraq as the direct result of the personal crusade orchestrated by Lawrence and his allies.

In all three pieces, Lawrence used the crisis in Iraq as the starting point of his argument. In words that could be used today, he criticized the British government for an appalling lack of follow-through in Iraq.

Lawrence accuses,

> The people of England have been led in Mesopotamia into a trap from which it will be hard to escape with dignity and honor. They have been tricked into it by a steady withholding of information. The Baghdad communiqués are belated, insincere, incomplete. Things have been far worse than we have been told, our administration more bloody and inefficient than the public knows. It is a disgrace to our imperial record, and may soon be too inflamed for an ordinary cure. We are to-day not far from disaster.[4]

Evidently, our own age is not the only one in which people heard what they wanted to hear, with predictably disastrous consequences.

Lawrence goes on to blame the government for not forcing its administrators in Iraq to come clean about what was happening, which began as its failure to exercise due diligence with Wilson's administration.

"The cabinet cannot disclaim all responsibility. They receive little more news than the public: they should have insisted on more, and better. They have sent draft after draft of reinforcements, without enquiry."[5] Faulting the government for seeing only a short-term military hiccup, Lawrence makes clear here that the underlying problem is political and that only an entirely new way of looking at developing peoples will allow London escape from the very large hole it had dug for itself.

Lawrence made plain in all three articles that it was at root Britain's threadbare top-down imperial philosophy that was the primary cause of its misfortunes in Iraq and throughout the Empire. In the *Times* piece, he wrote, "It is not astonishing that their [Iraqi] patience has broken down after two years. The government we have set up is English in fashion, and is conducted in the English language. So it has 450 British executive officers running it, and not a single responsible Mesopotamian. In Turkish days 70 percent of the executive civil service was local. Our eighty thousand troops there are occupied in police duties, not in guarding the frontiers. They are holding down the people."[6]

Explicitly Lawrence makes it clear that the British administration, with its emphasis on top-down control, is proving more repressive than the previous Turkish government, a fact designed to provoke liberal imperialists, already aghast at the government's brutal repression of the revolt. In the *Observer,* Lawrence continues in this vein, comparing British action in Mesopotamia with French brutality in Syria: "It would show a lack of humor if we reproved them [France] for a battle near Damascus [Maysalun], and the blotting out of the Syrian essay in self-government, while we were fighting battles near Baghdad, and trying to render the Mesopotamians incapable of self-government, by smashing every head that raised itself among them."[7] What the situation requires, he wrote, was nothing less than "a tearing up of what we have done, and beginning again on advisory lines."[8]

Lawrence's articles cleverly appealed to both liberal and conservative imperialists. To liberal imperialists he underlined the repressive nature of running such a dysfunctional system, and included reminders that Britain had broken its word to the Arabs regarding self-determination. Given the systemic crisis, the only immediate alternative, as he put it, "seems to be conquest, which the ordinary Englishman does not want, and cannot afford."[9]

To the conservatives, he argued that things would only get worse financially: "The expense curve will go up to 50 million pounds for this financial year, and yet greater efforts will be called for from us as the Mesopotamian desire for independence grows."[10] He was appealing to the conservative distaste for throwing good money after bad. But he did hold out hope to conservative imperialists, wryly commenting at the end of the *Observer* article that his advisory view of imperialism ought to be adopted, "with a hoot of joy, because it will save us a million pounds a week."[11] While the number was certainly exaggerated, Lawrence had pressed his fiscal point home with conservative imperialists.

With the liberals, Lawrence adopted a more passionate tone. In the climax of his *Times* piece, Lawrence stirringly argues, "The Arabs rebelled against the Turks during the war not because the Turk government was notably bad, but because they wanted independence. They did not risk their lives in battle to change masters, to become British subjects or French citizens, but to win a show of their own."[12]

Linking this passionate desire for independence to broken British promises, he says of the Mesopotamian insurrection, "We are told the object of the rising was political, we are not told what the local people want. It may be what the [British] Cabinet has promised them."[13]

To this unseemly example of British duplicity, Lawrence further exercised liberal imperialists by laying bare the brutal tactics that had been used to quell the revolt. Employing the deadly logic of dominance to ironic effect, he deadpanned, "By gas attacks the whole population of offending districts could be wiped out neatly; and as a method of government it would be no more immoral than the present system."[14] In pulling back the curtain of imperial rule, Lawrence exposed to liberal imperialists the necessary brutality that lay behind the scenes, a prerequisite for keeping the faithless British system going. For many of the "lost generation" such as Lawrence, this was indeed not the cause for which they had so recently, and so valiantly, fought.

Lawrence could offer a real world example of how an alternative Arab administration ought to be run: Feisal's independent kingdom in Syria, doomed only by outside colonial forces, rather than from within. Before news of Maysalun reached London, Lawrence wrote in the *Times,* "Feisal's government in Syria has been completely independent for two years, and has maintained public security and public services in its area."[15] This self-sustaining government looked particularly good, compared with the shambles of Mesopotamia. Even after Feisal's ouster by the French, Lawrence contrasted Greater Syria's possibilities with the dire situation in Baghdad. Lawrence hoped that here was a model, and a man, worth resurrecting.

Lawrence was unequivocal in saying that the India Office and its representative in Mesopotamia, Arnold Wilson, was the villain of the piece. Painting Wilson as an incompetent, Lawrence compared his stewardship of Mesopotamia with more successful British rule in Egypt:

"Cromer [the former Consul-General in Cairo] controlled Egypt's six million people with five thousand British troops; Colonel Wilson fails to control Mesopotamia's three million with ninety thousand troops."[16]

This personal attack, designed to galvanize public opinion against Wilson, came on the eve of Lawrence's bureaucratic battle with the India Office. Lawrence makes it clear who is his ally in his crusade to overturn British imperial policy: the formidable Winston Churchill, then secretary for war in Lloyd George's cabinet. Lawrence saw Churchill as an ally, due to the fact that he was calling for the troop reductions that made Lawrence's stakeholder approach the only viable new policy option for a retrenching British Empire. Lawrence makes clear, "The War Office [under Churchill] has made every effort to reduce our forces, but the decisions of the Cabinet have been against them."[17] By showing that Churchill favored cost-cutting and using the popular issues of economy and troop reduction, Lawrence was trying to elevate Churchill while denigrating Wilson in the court of public opinion. The alliance of these two extraordinary men was at hand.

Finally, Lawrence laced his articles with proactive and specific policy alternatives for the government to adopt. He was not merely a skeptic of present government policy; he answered the universal question that policymakers ask their critics: "What would you do instead?" Using his celebrity and unquestioned position as the preeminent British expert on the Middle East, Lawrence made clear his alternative policy for Mesopotamia.

In the *Times,* Lawrence proposed that over the next 12 months, Britain should make Arabic the governing language of Mesopotamia. thus decreasing the number of senior British administrators in the country, as most were not native speakers. This would allow the rehiring of quality Arab staff to the government. Second, Arab troops should be trained and given policing responsibilities for the country. Echoing his views in "The New Imperialism" about the ultimate status of the country, Lawrence added, "we should then hold of Mesopotamia exactly as much (or as little) as we hold of South Africa or Canada. I believe the Arabs in these conditions would be as loyal as anyone in the Empire, and they would not cost us a cent."[18]

By advocating local political control with London retaining authority over foreign affairs, much as Britain had done over the nineteenth century with white settler dominions such as South Africa, Canada, and Australia, Lawrence now sought to give the entire formerly top-down colonial system of the Middle East, Africa, and India, a similar, more decentralized status. Lawrence saw this as the only way to place the Empire as a whole, on a more solid and sustainable footing.

However, at this moment of supreme opportunity, there were early criticisms of Lawrence's approach that went largely unnoticed. In an August 3, 1920 letter to the *Times* written by a Captain Tytler, who had served in Iraq during the past three years, he cautioned against following Lawrence's lead. Tytler noted that Lawrence knew little about Mesopotamia and pointed out that placing the Shia majority under a Sunni prince such as Feisal, an option that was finding increasing favor in the government, would offend the Shia and lead to lasting tensions. Conservative MP and Iraqi veteran Colonel Freemantle asked in the House of Commons if there was any evidence of local support for a Sunni prince from the Hejaz running Iraq.[19]

Ironically, Lawrence's skeptics were attacking him using his own ideas, that local legitimacy mattered above all in nation building, that political outcomes must correspond to the local unit of politics, and that detailed cultural knowledge of the state was essential if it was to be transformed. Sadly, this cogent critique went unheeded in Lawrence's rush to make things right for Feisal.

There is little doubt that the Iraq crisis, and Lawrence's letter writing crusade that followed, turned the bureaucratic tide in his favor. As more and more politicians began coming around to his point of view, Lawrence was to reenter the governmental arena, joining the one-of-a-kind Winston Churchill in trying to radically change British imperial policy. But something would be lost along the way. Lawrence jettisoned his own enlightened governing philosophy, devised in the cauldron of the Great War, in order to win a throne, any throne, for Feisal.

Chapter 8

"One more such victory, and we shall be undone."

—King Pyrrhus of Epirus, after winning the
Battle of Asculum, 279 B.C., at great cost

In 1919, during the Paris Peace Conference, Winston Churchill
invited T. E. Lawrence to lunch. Churchill, who himself had first
gained notoriety as an escaped POW during the Boer War, was
eager to meet the famous hero of the desert. Ironically, their first
meeting produced a minor argument. Churchill, a staunch monar-
chist, had disapproved of Lawrence's recent decision not to accept
the decorations offered by George V, and told him so. But after lis-
tening to Lawrence explain the reasons for his gaudy refusal,
Churchill was won over; he came away from their meeting impressed
by Lawrence's moral courage. Thus began a friendship that lasted for
the rest of Lawrence's life.

In many ways Churchill and Lawrence were a well-suited pair. Politically, both men produced extreme reactions, particularly among the
many who were less talented then they. Both were physically brave, men
of action, who yet aspired to be taken seriously as great writers. Both
were visionaries, whose manic depressive tendencies left them either

bounding around with unquenchable energy or lying inert, in despair. Contemporaries thought of both men as brilliant yet recklessly dangerous. They were intellectual; adventurous (both had traveled the world); bookish, yet practical, war heroes with an idealized view of what the British Empire could be.

Churchill thought Lawrence one of the greatest men of the age and was a little awe-struck by his younger friend, a reaction that bemused Churchill's contemporaries. Churchill described Lawrence at the time they met in Paris: "From amid the flowing draperies his noble features, his perfectly-chiseled lips and flashing eyes loaded with fire and comprehension shone forth. He looked what he was, one of Nature's greatest princes."[1] This hero-worship was coupled with Churchill's total respect for Lawrence's point of view regarding Middle Eastern affairs. In Churchill, Lawrence had finally found his principal ally in his crusade to make things finally right with Feisal.

Lawrence symbolized everything that Churchill personally believed in. He was a scholar who was as at home in the chanceries of Europe as on the battlefield. Displaying exceptional valor in war, Lawrence was also passionately committed, albeit in his own way, to the idea of Empire that was central to Churchill's thinking about Britain's role in the world. By so wholly charming Churchill, Lawrence was able to place the formidable War Office that Churchill ran behind his schemes to remake British colonial policy.

Since the end of the war, the two friends had been working on parallel lines. Churchill had been the cabinet's severest critic of Lloyd George's Middle East policy. As minister for war he warned that post–Great War Britain did not have the troops and that Parliament did not have the money to pursue an imperial policy of coercion in the region.

That put him philosophically very close to Lawrence who in turn provided Churchill with the alternative policy with which to challenge the status quo.

On a more personal level, Churchill accepted Lawrence's point that Britain did indeed owe Feisal a moral debt. This was be no small factor in the calculations and policies Churchill would soon promote as colonial secretary.

Lawrence returned Churchill's affection, and he would often argue with his closest friends, the socialist playwright George Bernard Shaw and his wife Charlotte, about the merits of the conservative Churchill. In the 1920s, when Churchill was waging a losing campaign for parliament, Lawrence came out of his self-imposed exile to write a letter to the *Daily Express,* extolling Churchill, "The man's as brave as six, as good-humored, shrewd, self-confident, & considerate as a statesman can be: & several times I've seen him chuck the statesmanlike course & do the honest thing instead."[2] Lawrence said of Churchill that he was "a great man," for whom he felt, "not merely admiration, but a very great liking."[3]

With Churchill working from inside the government and Lawrence galvanizing public opinion, the two, in the latter half of 1920, were to stage a successful assault on the British imperial structure.

Following the Indian Mutiny of 1857, the rulers of the British Empire had adopted as conventional wisdom a centralized view of the political control of its colonies. It was thought that it had been a lack of direct control that had encouraged Britain's anti-imperialist enemies to rise up on the subcontinent, causing the greatest British colonial crisis of the nineteenth century. Following the Great War they were merely reverting to centralizing form in Iraq.

In one sense, Lawrence's postwar bureaucratic battle signaled the final showdown between the old philosophy underlying nineteenth century British imperialism, epitomized by Arthur Wilson and Foreign Secretary Lord Curzon, which looked upon Asia and Africa as regions to be economically manipulated or carved up for the greater good of London, and "The New Imperialism" of Lawrence and his Arab Bureau colleagues, who dreamed of Arab independence within the overall unity of the British Empire.

Lawrence found his most implacable critics in the India Office, who were supporters of the old school of imperialism. They had been a thorn in Lawrence's side regarding almost every issue relating to the Middle East. They supported Ibn Saud, a rival warlord and founder of today's Saudi Arabia, over Feisal's father Hussein in Arabia. They favored direct British rule over "The New Imperialism." Whenever French interests conflicted with Arab concerns, the India Office favored Paris. They were skeptical of the policy of promoting the Hashemite family, which was a cornerstone of Lawrence's efforts to make things right with Feisal. In Arnold Wilson, schooled in the ways of the India Office and temporary ruler of the lands of Iraq, Lawrence found his most objectionable opponent.

Wilson was desperate to maintain the old imperialism, even if it meant thwarting or downright disobeying orders from London. Wilson ignored even his India Office colleagues when he felt they were wavering on the core tenets of imperialism. In June 1920, in an attempt to rein him in, the India Office instructed Wilson to issue a proclamation to the people of Mesopotamia of the intention of the British government to establish an Arab Council of State under an Arab president, and prepare a constitution for the country, after consulting local elites. When Wilson published the decree he omitted the word "Arab" before "Council" and failed to mention that local elites should be consulted before a constitution was drafted, effectively sabotaging the initiative.

Wilson's behavior was extreme; but he was not alone in his views. Sir Arthur Hirtzel, the powerful assistant under-secretary of state for the India Office and Wilson's ally, thought the Arabs, "no more capable of administering severally or collectively than the Red Indians."[4] This was the classic top-down British Imperial position. Further, Hirtzel always favored French over Arab interests, for the simple reason that the French were a greater national interest priority for Britain. As he put it, with the French, "we have to live and work . . . all over the world."[5]

Both the India Office in London and the Viceregal government in Delhi had long seen Mesopotamia as a future colony. Certainly the India Office felt that at a minimum, the Ottoman provinces of Basra and Baghdad were geographically within its sphere of influence, believing that they were natural extensions of the subcontinent's frontier. While it administered Mesopotamia (which included southern Basra and central Baghdad, but not the northern Kurdish region) in clunky partnership with the Foreign and War Offices, the India Office expected, and under Wilson, was given, the lead role in running the country. This situation proved abhorrent to those in Arab Bureau such as Hogarth, Allenby, and Storrs, who disapproved of its paternalistic approach to governing.

The India Office was on more solid ground in attacking Hashemite claims to rule in the region. In the bureaucratic battle between Lawrence and Churchill and the India Office in the latter part of 1920, Lawrence's foes made it clear they preferred Ibn Saud, a rival Arabian chieftain with concrete ties to Mesopotamia over Feisal as a possible ruler for the country. Ironically, the India Office opposed the Hashemites for the most Lawrence-like of reasons; they had no real historical, political, or cultural connection with the country and thus lacked legitimacy there. As the goal of a throne for Feisal once again appeared to be within reach, Lawrence was to conveniently forget the bottom-up philosophy that had made their partnership so dynamic in the first place.

The Wilson controversy was only a part of the larger Middle Eastern puzzle for the British. Lawrence and Churchill saw Wilson as the symptom of the failures of British policy in the Middle East rather than the cause, believing the expensive paternalistic philosophy he and his allies espoused was the root problem, explaining Britain's failures in the region.

Traditionally the Foreign Office and the India Office were the two competing bodies that dealt with the Arabic-speaking portions of the Ottoman Empire. Virtually everyone agreed that this arrangement had to be refined. Determined that the bureaucratic infighting over colonial policy between the Foreign, India, and War Offices must come to an end, the two set out to wage bureaucratic war on the British elite, arguing that the Colonial Office (presumably with Churchill at its head) should have primary control over Mesopotamia, and that power be concentrated in one British cabinet department.

These maneuverings masked two distinct policy questions about Iraq that needed an immediate answer: should power there be devolved or should the British continue to push on with direct rule? Should a Hashemite prince be appointed as head of Iraq or should another more suitable leader be found to lead the country? There was a complicated overlap between the bureaucratic and policy-driven puzzles, with Lawrence and Churchill arguing for the Colonial Office, some form of devolution, and Feisal against the India Office's preference for the status quo. These two extremes bracketed the bureaucratic infighting over colonial issues in the waning days of Lloyd George's premiership.

But beyond these policy differences, this was also a contest between two men—Lawrence and his arch rival, Wilson. Hubert Young, Lawrence's wartime comrade in the Arab Revolt and a leading member of the Foreign Office's Eastern Department, put it this way, "Our policy in the Middle East during the last 3 or 4 years has been very largely influenced—I will not say controlled—by two strong personalities. On the Syrian side we have had Colonel Lawrence, encouraging Arab aspirations . . . On the Mesopotamian side we have had Sir Arnold Wilson checking the same aspirations and making no effort to disguise his reasons for doing so."[6]

Lawrence had his celebrity, the press, and public opinion on his side. He also had the support of a group of primarily Conservative MPs who had worked with him in the Great War. Lord Winterton, Aubrey Herbert, and William Ormsby-Gore all fundamentally agreed with him that British colonial policy needed a substantial overhaul and should be vested in one British cabinet department. Lawrence also had direct access to, and the broad sympathy of, the direct decision-makers on the Middle East question—the prime minister, Foreign Secretary Curzon, and Winston Churchill—in pushing for Feisal to be made king of Iraq. Wilson had nothing like this public or bureaucratic firepower.

On the contrary, Wilson's insubordination caused his colleagues to distance themselves from him, a process that gained momentum as the Iraqi insurrection flared. Lashing out for someone else to blame for the insurrection in Mesopotamia, Wilson did himself no favors by turning to conspiracy theories, hysterically accusing Feisal's government in Syria of somehow fomenting the explosion there, all the while admitting evidence proving his point did not exist.

Even Arthur Hirtzel, had admonished Wilson, "Lord Curzon [the foreign secretary] is especially always on the theme of not governing Mesopotamia as if it were an Indian province, which is what he suspects you of doing."[7] Wilson failed to heed Hirtzel's warnings, and so, beginning in August 1919, even before the insurrection, Hirtzel began suggesting that the more temperate Sir Percy Cox, who knew Mesopotamia well from his time spent as chief political officer in the British colonial army in the region during the war, be appointed as Civil Commissioner for Baghdad. Cox had been sent off temporarily to secure British imperial interests in Persia, but would be available for his new assignment sometime in the autumn of 1920. Similarly, in the Foreign Office, Lord Curzon had Hubert Young draw up a memo detailing the Foreign Secretary's consistent opposition to Wilson's administration since April 1919.

By June 1920, even the India Office had had enough of Wilson. In a June 16th meeting, Lord Edwin Montagu, the secretary of state for India, admitted that "he had never held the view that Colonel Wilson, with his marked inclination to concentrate power in his own hands, could fairly be asked to carry out the policy [of the Lloyd George government]."[8] The very next day, without even securing the bureaucratic support of his own department, the cabinet decided Cox should replace

Wilson. Thus even before the insurrection he had done so much to bring about, Wilson was on his way out the door.

*H*ousting the arrogant Wilson proved easy, there remained in the latter part of 1920 a genuine bureaucratic dogfight over which cabinet department should control Middle East policymaking.

At the end of World War I, the Foreign Office had supported the pro-Hashemite views of Lawrence and the Arab Bureau, while the India Office supported its ally Ibn Saud. The incoherence of this arrangement reached ludicrous proportions in May 1919, when at the battlefield of Turaba in Arabia, the two Arab chieftains' forces came to blows. Ibn Saud won the battle, sending Hussein's son and the commander in the field Abdullah scurrying back toward the Hejaz. In a panic, the Foreign Office appealed to General Allenby to right the strategic situation by threatening to send tanks to the aid of the Hashemites. At the last moment, the India Office advised Ibn Saud to retreat. But for one ridiculous instant it looked as if the British taxpayer would be fronting the cost for a proxy war between two feuding cabinet departments of their own government.

Churchill argued that this could not continue, if Britain was ever to have a coherent colonial policy. He further believed that this duplication of effort was not an expense that should be borne by the hardpressed British taxpayer. He suggested that a new Middle Eastern department be established within the Colonial Office to manage Palestine, Transjordan, and Iraq.

While Curzon and the Foreign Office supported the ouster of Wilson and favored more devolution and Feisal as ruler of Mesopotamia, they certainly wished to remain at the controls. Curzon was therefore strongly against Churchill's plan.

Lord Curzon had already been one of the dominating personalities in British politics for decades. As with Lawrence and Winston Churchill, few people who knew him were neutral about him; he was by nature a polarizer. A horseback riding accident when he was a teenager had left him with a debilitating spinal injury. He was in pain all his adult life, often overcome with insomnia, which did not help his demeanor or his personality. Arrogant, stiff, eloquent, and brilliant, he had traveled widely in his youth, making the most of his aristocratic family's immense fortune. He visited Russia, Central Asia, Persia, Siam, French Indochina, Korea, and Afghanistan, and his first-hand knowledge of those places gave his speeches on foreign policy authority. Always fascinated by the East, he was, like Churchill and Lawrence, a committed imperialist, if of a more conventional variety.

The crowning achievement of Curzon's career had come early; he had been Viceroy of India from 1899 to 1905, reaching the exalted position at the tender age of 39. His tenure had been a great success, and it was predicted that he would soon be prime minister. But his career had stalled, blocked by both his legion of enemies and the Liberal ascendancy that put in power former Prime Minister Asquith, as well as Lloyd George.

To keep balance in Lloyd George's grand coalition, the Conservative Curzon had been made foreign secretary. However, in this role, he proved a disappointment. He never had the prime minister's support;

Lloyd George saw him as overly pompous, self-important, and hopelessly overrated. When it came to the bureaucratic showdown with Churchill and Lawrence, Curzon did not find himself in a strong position. As Lawrence put it, "Curzon is of course the enemy; but he's not a very bold enemy."[9]

On the last day of 1920, Lloyd George finally acted. He was determined to put an end to the disastrous rivalry between Curzon's Foreign Office and Edwin Montagu's India Office. By now, following the Iraqi insurrection, Churchill and Lawrence were pushing on an open door, as the country and much of the British elite were with them. Churchill argued that the Colonial Office should control policy-making in the Middle East, while Lord Curzon urged that his Foreign Office should play the primary role. Lord Montagu, himself a decentralizer running an India Office whose ethos favored direct rule, was happy to give way. Even within its ranks of convinced paternalists, the dispirited India Office mandarins made no effort to retain their position in Baghdad, as by now, given the chaos of the revolt, they were glad to rid themselves of Iraq.

That there was a great bureaucratic struggle within the government can be seen by the fact that the prime minister called for a vote on the issue by the full cabinet, something that he rarely did. By a vote of eight to five, Churchill and Lawrence bested their rivals; the Colonial Office had won. While the Foreign Office retained control over policy-making in Egypt, Syria and Persia, the Colonial Office was placed in direct charge of British policy in Mesopotamia, Arabia, and Palestine. The India Office had been effectively shut out of Middle East colonial decision-making.

The very next day, January 1, 1921, Lloyd George offered Churchill the position of colonial secretary. On January 7, Lawrence became his first appointment to the new Middle East Department of the Colonial

Office, as Special Adviser on Arab Affairs, reporting to Churchill. After the despair of Damascus, and the treachery of Versailles, Lawrence had re-emerged to finally possess the political power necessary to keep faith with his Arab comrades from the Desert Revolt.

In the meantime, Feisal was emerging as a consensus choice for the position of king of Iraq, a country which would formally unite Mesopotamia with the Kurdish *sanjak* to its north. Lloyd George, Churchill, Lawrence, Curzon, and all their allies were firmly committed to his candidacy. About the only sour note was struck by internal India Office complaints. Regarding Lawrence's untiring advocacy of Feisal, the India Office stiffly noted, "[W]ithout in the least willing to deprecate Colonel Lawrence's achievements and undoubted genius, it must be said about him that he does not at all represent—and would not I think, claim to represent—the local views of northern Mesopotamia [Kurdistan] and Iraq."[10]

While it was certainly rich to see the India Office resort to arguing in favor of a local Iraqi political opinion they cared little for, unfortunately, the fact that their comments amounted to bureaucratic sour grapes does not mean that they were not correct. Like Tytler, Freemantle, and other early critics, the India Office was coherently using Lawrence's stakeholder philosophy against him. The two policy goals Lawrence and Churchill had—to give Iraqis more control over choosing their government and making things right with Feisal—were fatally contradictory. Something was going to have to give.

The most logical policy was to move from direct, heavy-handed rule to an indirect position of dominance, picking a pliable Arab ruler to keep

Iraq quiet at far less cost. Churchill had moved from the War Office to the Colonial Office to accomplish precisely this; his imperative was to radically cut costs while keeping the commitments of empire. Churchill announced, "that everything else that happens in the Middle East is secondary to the reduction in expense."[11] By September 1922, Churchill had reduced British expenditure in the Middle East by 75 percent, from 45 million to 11 million pounds per annum.

Devolution was a strategy suddenly in vogue across the Empire. Allenby, now the British high commissioner in Cairo, pushed the policy of the New Imperialism there, whereby the Egyptians would take charge of their own domestic affairs, while the British continued to run foreign policy. Allenby was able to use his great prestige to counter significant Whitehall opposition. His proposals were accepted February 28, 1922.

Lawrence was now in a perfect position to promote devolution in Iraq. Hubert Young, his wartime comrade and a personal friend of Feisal's, now headed the political and administrative branch of the Colonial Office's new Middle Eastern Department. He entirely agreed with Lawrence's policy prescriptions for Iraq, devolution, and Feisal. But Young was Lawrence's boss in name only. Lawrence was the most important adviser to the new Colonial Secretary; Churchill invariably deferred to his opinion, even where the rest of the new Middle Eastern Department might not agree.

By now, Feisal's candidacy had picked up enough momentum that, when it came to it, even Montagu and Arnold Wilson gave him their support. Ominously, Wilson wrote that emir seemed like a good solution to the Iraq problem given that, "the Syrian experience had taught Feisal compromise with the British and to be wary of Arab nationalists."[12] Wilson had not changed his overall view of the world. Rather, he was dimly beginning to see that nothing in Feisal's election meant that

Britain might not still dominate Iraq. Conversely, Feisal might indeed serve well as cover; a seemingly independent Arab king who in reality was wholly dependent on British power and goodwill to remain in charge.

In December 1920, just half a year after his defeat on the road to Damascus, Feisal came to Britain. At a lengthy meeting at the home of Lord Winterton, a Conservative MP, he was discretely asked (for Britain was somewhat concerned about the French reaction to their plans) how he would react if offered the Iraqi throne by Britain. Feisal refused at first, as he suspected that he would be little more than an imperial pawn. Having no shame, British officials enlisted Lawrence to persuade Feisal to accept the throne.

In the end, Feisal accepted the crown, but only if he were allowed to actually govern, having primary control over the country's affairs, and only if his brother Abdullah renounced his claims to the throne in Baghdad. Worryingly, and very much in contradiction with Lawrence's brilliant philosophy, the Iraqi people, the locals who were to be governed, were not consulted in any way, let alone thought about, in crafting this arrangement.

Worse still, Feisal never really would be able to govern independently in Iraq, whatever the British promised, since there he lacked the glorious elixir of legitimacy that he had possessed in Syria. Without local support he would never be perceived as much more than a British imperial puppet. Both Lawrence and the emir, in order to right Feisal's immediate fortunes, had willfully forgotten about the very principle that had underwritten their success in the desert—that above all, local legitimacy was necessary in order to forge a nation where one had not existed.

In February 1921, after only a month in office, Churchill announced that there would be an imperial conference in Cairo in another month's time to determine Britain's future policy in the Middle East. But, as is often the case in international diplomacy, the conference was merely a formality; decisions that would be ratified there had been made beforehand. Lawrence later claimed, "The decisions of the Cairo conference were prepared by us [Churchill and Lawrence] in London, over dinner tables at the Ship Restaurant in Whitehall."[13]

This was to prove the problem. Lawrence, so close to achieving his goal of placing the wronged Feisal on a throne, any throne, had began to behave as any standard top-down British imperialist might. In defiance of his life's work, sitting thousands of miles away, he was now determining outcomes for other peoples of whom he knew little.

Chapter 9

"On a hot Sunday afternoon, I created Transjordan."

—Winston Churchill, regarding the Cairo
conference of March 1921

As the present exercise in Iraqi nation building began to go wrong, there was a flurry of interest in the history surrounding the British establishment of the state in the 1920s. This was mostly used by proponents of the Iraqi adventure to try to save their intellectual reputations. They tended to point out the obvious fact that the Bush administration had failed miserably in its execution of an Iraqi nation-building strategy. The cause of nation building in general and in Iraq in particular remained just, if only the administration had not proved so incompetent. For instance, Niall Ferguson demanded, "Couldn't Tony Blair have lent the president the letters of Gertrude Bell?"[1]

The somewhat haughty implication is that if only the Americans had learned the hard-won lessons of the imperial master, Great Britain, all would have come right in Baghdad. This is worse than self-serving history; it is almost entirely wrong. For the Cairo Conference of March 1921 that established Iraq went almost entirely against the principles

Lawrence had laid out for working with developing peoples attempting to build a nation.

Feisal had no specific knowledge of Iraq and its people, and the British almost wholly ignored or worked against local Iraqi culture and the politics that flowed from it. The emir was kept in power by military means, without either his regime or the British paying attention to the political and psychological factors necessary to make the monarchy self-sustaining. The British ignored the local ethno-religious units of Iraqi politics, centered on the Sunni, Shia, and Kurdish communities, instead vainly trying to forge a unitary, centralized state.

In ordaining Feisal king, the British, not the Iraqis, were picking political winners and losers. As a result, the locals were not made stakeholders in the new monarchy, which never acquired the vital asset of local legitimacy. If people are to read Bell's letters, it must be to gather what not to do in terms of nation building, rather than as an intellectual guide.

Winston Churchill opened the Cairo conference on March 12, 1921. The purpose of the meeting was for the British to sort out the tensions in the Middle East following the unsatisfactory peace made immediately after the war. He had summoned forty of the foremost British experts on the Middle East whom he counted on to help him make his way through the thicket of regional politics. Churchill called them his "40 thieves," and they amounted to a Who's Who of the Empire. Allenby, Cox, Hubert Young, Jafar Pasha, Air Minister Lord Trenchard, Bell, and Lawrence ostensibly gathered to construct a new British imperial policy.

Since almost everyone at the meeting knew everyone else, the atmosphere was intimate and the meetings moved along smartly, certainly compared with Versailles. In many ways, it was more like a Great War reunion than a fraught effort to remake British policy. However, the Cairo conference was a rigged game. Lawrence and his ally Gertrude Bell had already stitched up the result, determining the fate of Mesopotamia, Jordan, and Kurdistan.

Having wholly converted Churchill to his views, Lawrence corresponded with his old friend Gertrude Bell, who was now a senior advisor to the British Civil Administrator and to the de facto viceroy in Iraq, Sir Percy Cox. The removal of Arnold Wilson had produced the added advantage for Lawrence of making Bell Cox's deputy, and she had quickly become his most important aide. Lawrence realized his luck, coordinating with her over the Cairo outcome. Between them, these two remarkable allies managed the conference, which made support for Feisal's family a cornerstone of British imperial policy.

Following Feisal's acceptance of the Iraqi throne in December 1920, in early 1921, before the Cairo Conference had been convened, through communications between London and Baghdad, it had already been arranged by Churchill, Lawrence, Cox, and Bell that this diplomatic maneuver should quickly become a political reality. It is hard to imagine a more top-down policy process. St. John Philby, a noted regional expert who was close to rival warlord Ibn Saud (and the father of the famous British double agent Kim Philby) and a critic of the Cairo conference, left little doubt as to who was calling the shots in Mesopotamia. In his autobiography, he bitterly noted that Bell, "exercised an excessive and almost messianic effect on his [Cox's] judgment and decisions when . . . physically present in his counsels."[2]

This, coupled with Lawrence's sway over Churchill, sealed the Cairo decisions before the conference began. Lawrence later admitted as much. As Lawrence wrote to his postwar confidante, Charlotte Shaw, about the conference in 1927, "In 1921 at the Cairo conference [Bell] swayed all the Mesopotamian British officials to the Feisal solution, while Winston and I swayed the English people."[3] The Lawrence-Bell alliance is the key to understanding the Cairo decisions. The Hashemite Kingdom of Iraq was largely their creation.

A photograph from the time illustrates something of Bell's mettle. During a break in the conference, Churchill insisted that Lawrence travel with him by camel to see the pyramids. Though sliding like a jellyfish from his mount and hurting his ankle, Churchill completed the ride by Lawrence's side. In the picture taken of the occasion, there to the colonial secretary's immediate left sits a composed Gertrude Bell, complete with dress and hat, astride a camel, looking entirely comfortable in the company of these other heroes of the Empire.

As the conference delegates lounged around the luxurious Semiramis Hotel in Cairo, where semi-tame lions wandered the grounds, Lawrence and Bell had already picked the diplomatic winners and losers. Having only recently bureaucratically defeated the old imperialists, Lawrence was keen to push his political advantage to the full.

On one level, this is all entirely understandable. Most successful conferences are merely ratifications of previous diplomatic bargains struck in private. Lawrence would have been foolish indeed not to press his bureaucratic victory, after suffering Britain's diplomatic duplicity regarding the plight of Feisal. However, by now this imperative to assuage his personal sense of honor had become an obsession.

The Cairo conference—45 intensive sessions with the delegate-experts—commenced Saturday morning, March 12, 1921, and ended less than two weeks later, on March 22. Although, as Lawrence wrote his eldest brother, "everybody Middle East is here,"[4] only a small number of the delegates exercised any real power. The key issue was economic: how to cut the costs of occupying Mesopotamia. Two principal subgroups were formed to explore ways to do so, a political committee and a military one.

The political committee was at the center of the Cairo process. It consisted of Churchill, Lawrence, Cox, Bell, and Hubert Young. Their first and most significant task was to ordain Feisal as king of the new Iraqi state, believing that he could act as a bulwark against further Arab revolts.

One of the first tasks the political committee set for itself was to figure out how Feisal's kingship could be imposed upon Iraq, as if his ascension to the throne could be squared with local political desires, without giving the impression to both the Iraqis and the wider world that he was primarily a British imperial puppet. Here the British were arguing about form rather than substance, how to overcome the "problem" of local legitimacy rather than genuinely to work with local leaders to find an organic political solution. It was to be Feisal. The question was how to massage this exercise in top-down imperialism.

Second, ignoring the provincial system of the Ottomans, which correctly recognized that the Kurds, Shia, and Sunnis made up differing units of politics in the Mesopotamian region, the British announced the creation of a unitary and centralized Iraq, run by an unrepresentative Feisal from the center in Baghdad, despite the fact that such a political construct had never before existed.

Churchill and Lawrence were initially against including the non-Arab Kurdish *sanjak* (province) in the new Iraqi state, in order to give the new Iraq at least some coherence, as a fledgling state which including the non-Arab Kurds was likely to be chronically unstable. They hoped to instead make Kurdistan an independent entity, creating a buffer zone between the Arabs in the newly created Iraq and their former Turkish overlords. They had no such qualms about combining the very different Shia-dominated *sanjak* of Basra with the Sunni-dominated *sanjak* of Baghdad to form the Iraqi state. By ignoring his own tenet that the West could not pick or fundamentally alter the unit of politics for a developing people, Lawrence made it extremely likely that Iraq, which flew in the face of all prior history, would prove a fractious and unnatural country.

However, in what amounted to their only significant setback at the conference, they failed to secure the assent of the other delegates for Kurdish independence. Instead, the oil-rich region was seen as providing a vital economic bounty for the new state to possess; also, setting up yet another government in the region would prove more costly than maintaining everything from Baghdad. Much against the will of its people, Kurdistan was soon to join the new country.

Lawrence and Churchill were right to fight to keep the non-Arab Kurds out of what would inevitably amount to an Arab-dominated country. The sad history of the region since bears testimony to their long-ago fears about Iraq's chances for internal coherence, should the Kurdish region be included in the new construct.

Churchill, Lawrence, and Bell had determined Iraq's shape and ethnic composition. They had decided who would lead it, how it would be governed, who would be its citizens, and established what would be its laws and institutions. This amounted to quintessential top-down nation building. The irony was that these "New Imperialists," dedicated to the principle that greater local control over politics would remake and reenergize the British Empire, in the end largely adopted the tired, failed policies of top-down nation-builders such as Curzon and Wilson, that they so disparaged. It was a mistake to be repeated many times over, up until the present day by the West.

As the conference opened, Churchill received word that Feisal's brother Abdullah, the man who Lawrence had first interviewed and found wanting as leader of the Arab Revolt, had placed himself at the head of an army of 2,000 Arab nationalists in Transjordan, straddling Greater Syria and Iraq. Abdullah, who in many respects had greater claim in Western eyes to the throne of Baghdad than his brother, as he had earlier been discussed as a possible leader of the country by the British pre-Versailles, threatened to undo the conference's work, especially if he attacked French-dominated Syria. The French, none too pleased that their enemy Feisal was about to reemerge as the king of a neighboring country to Syria, might well have felt that Abdullah's attack on its colony was the last straw, and violently objected to putting Feisal on the Iraqi throne.

Churchill skillfully defused the potential crisis, in effect by buying Abdullah off. He was made the interim ruler of Transjordan, on the condition that he promise not to harass the nearby French. In the end, Lawrence helped secure two thrones for King Hussein's sons. Ironically, this very on-the-spot bit of political improvisation is the one Cairo decision to have stood the test of time. Abdullah's great-grandson, King Abdullah II, today sits on the throne of Jordan.

The practical British reward for all of this imperial maneuvering was to be able to cut costs. In turning the formal administration of Iraq over to an Arab government under Feisal, the British hoped to with-draw ground troops from the country over the period of a year, instead relying on the far cheaper option of Lord Trenchard's RAF bombers to keep the peace if another revolt flared up. Aerial attacks had decisively ended the Iraqi insurrection in 1920, and both Lawrence and Churchill were enthusiastic adherents of the possibilities of air power taking the place of the costly garrisoning of large numbers of British troops in its colonies.

For while the Cairo Conference was undoubtedly stage-managed by Lawrence and Gertrude Bell, the other delegates, driven by the con-suming imperative of cutting costs for the hard-pressed British govern-ment and taxpayer, quickly fell into line around their thrifty proposals. The central question was: Would the new political settlement hold?

Thus it was at the Cairo conference, and not in Baghdad, that Feisal was truly anointed king of Iraq. Feisal was not locally elected in any way. On the way back from Cairo to London at the Egyptian city of Port Said, Lawrence secretly met Feisal, providing him with the details of the conference. He also let Feisal in on the British plan to provide window dressing for his ascension to the Iraqi throne, making it appear that the emir was the choice of the people, rather than a British impe-rial stooge.

First, the British pressured the elderly *naqib* (senior Sunni religious leader) of Baghdad, a man with a far better pedigree to be king of Iraq than the emir, to invite Fesial to tour the country. That this was stage-managed can be seen by the fact that Feisal was already aboard a ship steaming to Iraq when he received the supposedly spontaneous message. Feisal's desire to be king at all costs can hardly be doubted; he readily fell in with Britain's Cairo plans. His tour of the country, however, despite significant British efforts, did not produce the desired overwhelming popular reception that Fesial had been hoping would smooth his way to the throne. What is surprising is that he expected to be received with acclamation in the first place, given his total lack of cultural legitimacy. As Bell biographer Janet Wallach makes clear:

> "[Feisal] had never before set foot in Iraq; he knew little of the people he would rule, of the land over which he would reign, of the history he would inherit. He had no knowledge of Iraqi tribes, no friendships with their sheikhs, no familiarity with the terrain—the marshes in the south, the mountains in the north, the grain fields, the river life—and no sense of connection with its ancient past. He even spoke a different dialect of Arabic."[5]

His first state visit to what would prove to be his adopted country was met, according to the British officials of the time, with listlessness and a decided lack of enthusiasm by his soon-to-be subjects. It set an ominous tone for the future.

Nevertheless, London pressed relentlessly forward. On July 11, 1921, a British-controlled Arab Council of Ministers in Baghdad, not an indigenous constitutional assembly, asked him to be king. Prodded by the British to provide the window dressing of local legitimacy, the Council called for a national referendum to confirm their "choice" of Feisal. This dubious invitation was further sullied by being confirmed by a sham referendum, one that would have made the Baath Party, Iraq's future tyrannical rulers, proud. On August 18, it was announced by the Council that an incredible ninety-six percent of voters approved Feisal's election, despite the fact that the largest ethnic group in Iraq, the Shia, were almost wholly against the new government, rightly convinced it was merely a British front.

Having been confirmed by this shabby process, Feisal formally accepted the throne of Iraq on August 23, 1921. Gertrude Bell herself went so far as to design both Iraq's new flag, as well as Feisal's coronation ceremony. It is hard to think of a more naked act of top-down imperialism than this process. But, in the end, such political strong-arm tactics were to have disastrous consequences, as Fesial's regime never truly "took" with the Iraqi people; he never possessed the very quality of local acceptance that had underlined his great wartime success in the Arab Revolt. This lack of political legitimacy would perpetually haunt Feisal, as he was unable to practically rule a country where he was kept in power only by the tip of British bayonets.

At Cairo, the architects of the new Iraqi order had treated the Middle East as if it were some sort of *tabula rasa,* the attitude that was the hallmark of nineteenth century imperialism. But the forces released by President Wilson's failed dreams of self-determination would never again really dissipate. Lawrence had sold the Cairo package to Churchill, who had the political power to ram it through at the time. Lawrence and Churchill could not however, change facts on the ground, which was why the Cairo accords did not put the region on the firm path to stability, let alone make it a buttress of the British Empire.

When pressed by skeptics, accomplices to the Cairo Conference acknowledged the contradictions that lay behind it. Churchill, when announcing the Cairo decisions in the House of Commons on June 14, issued a contradictory statement that paid lip service to the fiction that Britain did not intend nor desire to force a particular ruler on the Iraqi people while at the same time endorsing Emir Feisal as "the most suit-able candidate in the field."[6] Churchill extolled Feisal, saying that he was "an ideal candidate [who had] very special qualifications for the post . . . He had himself fought gallantly on our [the British] side and had then taken part in the various exploits of desert warfare with which the name of Colonel Lawrence will always be associated."[7]

The first statement spoke to Lawrence's philosophy, the second to a very different political reality. For Churchill's praising of Feisal in no way explains how his sterling wartime qualities conferred local Iraqi po-litical legitimacy upon him. By now, for Churchill, Lawrence, and the British government, seating Feisal on the throne could best be explained by the desire to pay a debt, not by objective policy considerations. Like-wise, Sir Percy Cox, the true ruler of Iraq, when asked why Feisal should be king of a country about which he knew next to nothing, blandly an-swered that the sherif and his family had rendered His Majesty's Gov-ernment a valuable service. This was closer to the truth.

During Churchill's June 14 speech to the Commons, he omitted two very important details. He neglected to either mention that there was considerable opposition to Feisal's candidacy within the newly formed country, or the fact that he had a formidable rival, Sayid Talib, one with a good great deal of local support, who had been kidnapped and exiled by the British government to get him out of the way. Feisal's ascension was based on the perpetration of what can only be described as a crime.

Sayid Talib was the son of the prominent *naqib* of Basra. During the Great War, he had founded an Arab nationalist movement that

opposed the continuance of Turkish rule. Along the way, he acquired
a reputation for cunning, ruthlessness, and independence. As such,
Sir Percy Cox, then the chief political officer with the British army in
Mesopotamia, had deported Talib to India in 1916, as his loyalty to
the hard-pressed British cause was in question. Returning in 1917, he
reached a modus operandi with London, even acting for a time as
Mesopotamian minister of the interior. But it was always a marriage
of convenience. Talib supported the British over the Turks only inso-
far as he believed they were likely to keep their promise of granting the
region full independence after the war.

Before his 1920 ouster, Arnold Wilson had suggested that Talib
might be a possible candidate for the throne. But when it became clear
that the British, in the local guise of Gertrude Bell, favored Fesial for the
crown, Talib grew more outspoken. From his base in the important city
of Basra, Talib reached a provisional agreement with the fading, elderly,
Naqib of Baghdad that he would support him for the throne, in return
for a chance at the succession after his demise.

Talib toured the country, coining the nationalist slogan, "Iraq for
the Iraqis," stressing his own Mesopotamian roots as opposed to Feisal's
far-away pedigree. Meeting with local tribal leaders and making countless impassioned speeches about Arab independence, he accepted the
need to cooperate with the British even as he objected to their med-
dling in Iraq's choice of a ruler. British intelligence officers reported with
great consternation that Talib was getting a magnificent reception; there
is little doubt that he possessed a degree of local legitimacy far superior
to that of Feisal.

Cox, commenting on all this in early 1921, noted in reports back
to London that Talib "put forward the claims of an Iraqi ruler for Iraq.

There are indications that this claim receives a considerable measure of support, and there is I think no question but that Feisal's candidature will be strongly resisted."[8] Worse, Talib posed a mortal threat to general British designs, as by his nationalist pronouncements he was putting into question the very legitimacy of British imperial control.

Something had to be done. Quickly, the British found a pretext for silencing the dangerous Talib. At a dinner party for the correspondent of the British newspaper, the *Daily Telegraph,* Talib was heard to say that if the British were not fair about the candidates for the throne, if they were seen to actively take sides, the Iraqi tribes might rise in revolt. This statement can be read as either objective political analysis, or as a threat. The British conveniently viewed it as the latter, as this allowed them to remove the troublesome nationalist. They proceeded to kidnap the one candidate for the throne who had the best claim to local legitimacy.

Sir Percy Cox invited Talib to a formal tea party at his residence in mid-April 1921. When he arrived, Talib found that Cox was curiously absent, leaving his wife, Lady Cox, to entertain his guests. Gertrude Bell was among those present. Cakes were served and tea was poured. As he left the curious gathering, Talib bid good-bye to both Lady Cox and Bell. He was driven away from the British residence, only to be arrested just down the road by a fellow guest, Major Bovill, on the orders of Cox, his absent host.

Exiled to Ceylon, Talib was forbidden from returning to Iraq. Cox used the pretext of Talib's supposed threat to justify the deportation on the grounds of preserving law and order in the country. The British had rid itself of a significant nuisance, but under very shady circumstances.

It is little wonder that Churchill chose not to mention any of this during his speech to the Commons, putting forward the outcome of the recent Cairo conference. The message he wanted to leave with his fellow parliamentarians with was one of a problem solved, a crisis averted, a drain on the exchequer relieved. As a practical matter, the Cabinet had already approved the recommendations of the Cairo conference, on the condition that Feisal agreed not to use his new throne to undermine the French in Syria. Likewise, the Commons subsequently accepted the cabinet's Cairo recommendations, handing Churchill, Bell, and Lawrence a seemingly decisive political victory. However, it was to prove of the temporary variety.

Between 1918 and 1922, in London, Paris, Oxford, Cairo, and Amman, Lawrence struggled to fulfill what he considered to be his personal responsibility to the Arabs he had fought with during the war. This noble motive of friendship and fidelity led him to ignore his own philosophy of nation building, to the detriment of the world. However, now with the Cairo recommendations implemented and Feisal installed on the Iraqi throne, Lawrence felt that both he and his country had at last paid off its debt. Writing at the end of 1922, after retiring from public life into the seclusion he would never again leave, Lawrence wrote, "We were quit of our war-time Eastern adventure, with clean hands."[9] This moral cleansing had always been his personal driving force in the post-war era. Later, writing to his biographer, Robert Graves, in 1927, Lawrence described the Cairo settlement as, "the big achievement of my life."[10] For at the Semiramis Hotel, Lawrence believed he had finally been able to at last square the circle of balancing British imperial interests with those of his Arab friends.

He, along with Churchill and Bell, had changed the very nature of British foreign policy, relating to its colonies. Unlike the direct rule of the French throughout their empire, London would from now on try to accommodate moderate Arab nationalists through pursuing a policy of indirect rule over them.

That is what makes the failure of the whole endeavor so tragic. Mesopotamia was a country in which Lawrence had only the briefest first-hand experience. Ironically, this paltry first-hand knowledge amounted to even more than its new king possessed.

In normal circumstances, Fesial could easily be seen as the anti-Lawrence candidate for the throne. But alas, these were not normal circumstances.

Unlike in the Hejaz and Syria, where it was his very political legitimacy that gave the Arab Revolt credibility, Feisal was widely perceived in Iraq as merely a British stooge. As would prove true for the American occupiers decades on, he knew next to nothing about the country he was to rule. While Britain, unlike France, now favored ruling over its mandates as indirectly as possible, in line with Lawrence's urgings, in placing Feisal on the throne in Baghdad, because of the unique circumstances created by the debt Lawrence felt Britain owed him, they were artificially grafting a foreign, pro-British ruler onto captive peoples without their consent.

Beyond being intellectually lazy, it was untrue and politically disastrous for British officials to assume that because Feisal was an Arab he could naturally rule over any part of the region. In calling the peoples of the Middle East "Arabs," the West largely missed the point of the region's diversity. Egyptians, Arabians, Iraqis, and Syrians had very different histories, ethnic backgrounds, and dreams of the future. As the

Naqib of Baghdad tried to explain to an unlistening Gertrude Bell, "The Hejaz is one and the Iraq is one, there is no connection between them but that of the Faith [Islam]. Our politics, our trade, our agriculture, are all different from those of the Hejaz."[11] Lawrence had made his nation-building dream of natural, local, colonial growth buttressing the British Empire an impossibility by imposing an alien ruler upon the Iraqi people.

But this was just the first of the Cairo architects' mistakes when they decided upon a Hashemite solution to Mesopotamia's problems. As was the case with a later ruler of Iraq, Saddam Hussein, Feisal found himself the Sunni ruler of a largely Shia country. At the time, the three million people of Iraq were 50 percent Shia, 20 percent Sunni, 20 percent Kurd, and 10 percent amounting to a hodgepodge of Jews, Assyrians, Turkomen, Chaldean Catholics, and other Christians. The *Naqib* of Baghdad had not gone far enough in his warning to Gertrude Bell. True, Arabs were not one; but certainly neither were the Iraqis.

The long-time rulers of Mesopotamia, the Ottomans, had known better. They had divided the region up into the three separate provinces of Basra, Baghdad, and Mosul, respectively dominated by the Shia, the Sunnis, and the Kurds. Given that there was longstanding antipathy between Shia and Sunni Arabs, between the Arabs and the Kurds, between the various tribes, between the tribes and the city-dwellers, and a general resentment of the predominant Jewish commercial class in Baghdad, the odds that the new country would ever effectively pull together as a unified nation were always bound to be very low.

States not held together by the sinews of a common language, religion, geography, culture, ethnicity, and history, have not, with a few exceptions, fared well across the sands of time. Iraqis, with differing major ethnicities, practicing different forms of Islam, and with very different histories, were certainly far from a homogenous entity.

Given these impermeable realities, it is little wonder Iraq has not become a beacon of stability. As Daniel Byman wrote of recent American efforts to remake Iraq, "For now Iraqis remain loyal to their parochial leaders, not the central government."[12] To put it mildly, this has long been the case, as the primary units of politics in the region—the ethnic and/or religious groupings of Shia, Sunnis, and Kurds—have changed little over centuries.

At the time of Feisal's ascension to the throne, predictably the three groups had very different political yearnings. The Sunni nationalists wanted Iraq to emerge as an Arab kingdom, the Shia wanted Iraq to evolve into an Islamic religious state, and the Kurds in the north sought independence. This sounds frighteningly like today.

The British were warned on multiple occasions of their nation-building folly. John Van Ess, an American missionary and old Mesopotamian hand, explicitly warned his friend Gertrude Bell. "But Gertrude, you are flying in the face of four millenniums of history if you try to draw a line around Iraq and call it a political entity . . . They have never been an independent country."[13] Her response to this reasonable warning? "Oh, they will come around."[14]

Eight decades on, they still have not.

Given the minefield of diversity, it would have been almost impossible for the Iraq that emerged from Cairo to have provided the stability in the region that the British so desperately wanted. Given the heterogeneous nature of the place, only a political system in tune with this reality—a confederation of some sort, where a great deal of power was devolved locally—could have perhaps led to a happy outcome.

Instead, Lawrence and the British opted for the usual top-down, overly centralized solution that has remained a dubious hallmark of nation-building efforts up until today. Favoring the minority Sunnis, who comprised Feisal's ruling class, Lawrence and the British ensured that instability would plague the new Iraqi state, as the majority building block of the new country, the Shia, were consistently ignored. Further, domestic power was centralized in Baghdad, completely disregarding the heterogeneous political facts on the ground in Iraq.

This willful ignorance of the local political, social, and cultural realities of Iraq was in violation of Lawrence's entire philosophy. Its unnatural birth doomed the Iraqi state to perpetual turbulence from the start. In paying his debt, Lawrence had sacrificed what he believed. Doing the wrong thing for the right reasons was to have a catastrophic effect on Iraq for the rest of the century.

Lawrence's struggle had evolved into one primarily about his personal honor, repaying his debt to Feisal as English schoolboys are taught to do, rather than his advancing his general philosophy. It had become about him, rather than the people of Iraq, about his friend, rather than what would work in the long term. Was this deeply selfish or deeply honorable? History must accept the complexity of the man, saying it was both. But we are still experiencing the ruinous results; both specifically in Iraq and more generally in the loss of the only formula for nation building that stood a real chance of working throughout the twentieth century.

Chapter 10

"The edifice that has not firm foundations make not lofty; and if thou dost, tremble for it."

—Saadi (Persian poet)

I t would be nice if the story ended here, a triumphant vindication of friendship, high politics, and a remarkably enlightened political creed. However, history demands that we tell of things as they actually happened. The rest of the tale explains much of the reason for the chaos in the Middle East throughout the rest of the twentieth century, as well as the nightmare going on in Iraq today.

By sacrificing his ideals, Lawrence doomed the Hashemite project in Iraq to inglorious failure. Even worse, his brilliant strategy of bottom-up nation building, of making indigenous people the center of development efforts, became lost to time, ensuring that the ponderous, ineffective, top-down efforts at nation building would continue to bedevil the world until today.

The inadequacies of the Cairo conference loomed ever larger as the 1920s progressed. Feisal took the throne of Iraq not possessing any of the qualities that Lawrence believed were essential for political success.

Unlike in Syria, where Feisal's government had enjoyed real cultural and political legitimacy, in Iraq Feisal was an outsider. He was now merely a placeholder, reigning at the pleasure of the British power behind the throne. As has remained true today, outsiders picking political winners and losers is not the best way to establish political stability, or to quell the restive political spirit of the Iraqi peoples.

Lost in the romantic haze hovering over Hashemite era in Iraq is the incontrovertible fact that there were 30-plus coup attempts in the 30-plus years the family sat on the Iraqi throne, an average of more than one a year. To put it mildly, this was not a secure political system.

The reason for its failure was simple and should have been painfully obvious to Lawrence. Feisal's regime, and later that of his son and grandson, lacked from the outset, and never acquired, popular legitimacy. Feisal admitted that he owed his throne to Britain and needed its protection, recognizing that if they withdrew he would be immediately overthrown. As British Colonial Secretary Leo Amery noted, Feisal's writ extended only so far as did the power of British airplanes. If the planes were withdrawn the whole monarchy would inevitably fall to pieces.

The Anglo-Iraq Treaty symbolized his dependence. Forced on Feisal in 1922, in it Iraq agreed to "fully consult" with London regarding managing its finances and economy, ceded dominance over foreign and defense policy to Britain, put Britain in control of Iraq's oil wealth, and appointed British advisers to guide the king. It was pointed out that Feisal had no foreign minister in one of his early cabinets; instead "The [British] High Commissioner has, in effect, acted as Foreign Minister."[1] This level of British control was well beyond anything Lawrence had proposed.

Iraq began its existence burdened with a crippling debt to Britain. Ironically, Feisal's government was required to contribute to paying off a portion of the debt to the British that the hated Ottoman overlords had run up while they were in power. If Iraq attempted to shirk this onerous and patently unjust burden, the treaty allowed London to use military force in the country to collect it. The treaty became the symbol of Iraq's political subservience to Britain. In signing it, Feisal doomed himself and his heirs to being viewed domestically as nothing more than the agents of British control. Ironically, a younger generation of Arab nationalists was never to forgive this founder of modern Arab nationalism for seeming to sell out Iraqi sovereignty.

While Iraq was granted nominal independence and joined the League of Nations in 1932, the British retained control over the country's foreign and defense policy, as well as its economic policy. Jafar Pasha, Feisal's longtime associate, who ended up in the critical position of Iraqi Ambassador to the Court of St. James in London, defined Hashemite policy under the king as the "great task of welding his people into a nation and getting that nation to cooperate with Great Britain."[2] These priorities proved both hopelessly daunting and hopelessly contradictory. Feisal, the freedom fighter who had dreamt of a unified Arab state under his family's rule, died exhausted at a hotel in Berne, Switzerland, at the age of 50 in September 1933, little more than a placeholder for his former wartime allies.

Feisal's kingdom never became self-sustaining, the true mark of success for any nation-building effort. There were three Kurdish uprisings between 1922 and 1932, repression and consequent massacre of at least 3,000 of the Assyrian minority in 1933, and a southern rebellion by the Shia in 1935 and 1936. By 1950, the Jews had largely left the country following persecution due to the 1948 Arab-Israeli war. Throughout the life of the kingdom, 1921–1958, no less than 59 governments came to power, frequently, after 1936, through military coups.

Just before his death, Feisal openly wondered whether or not it was genuinely possible that Iraq could become a coherent nation. Its lack of cohesion led to the evolution of a political culture of strongmen, as it was thought that only decisive, centralized control could keep this fractious place together. The stage was set for the rise of Saddam Hussein, but he was merely the end result of a lengthy process that began with Lawrence.

The Iraqi pattern of government came to be characterized by international weakness and domestic centralized control, as regime after regime futilely tried to overcome the basic fact that Iraq was not a cohesive nation. For while its governments changed with bewildering speed, the same oligarchs dominated the scene throughout the Hashemite monarchy. Only 166 people served in cabinets over the 37 years of Hashemite rule; while governmental instability was rife, it was confined to a very small elite, which had little connection to the demographic realities of the country. For example, while the Shia made up 55 percent of the population at the time, they were, on average, represented in parliament by only 27 to 35 percent of the total membership. The ruling base skewed away from Iraq's demographic realities and was precariously narrow.

The Iraqi bicameral parliament, established in 1924, remained a farce in terms of representation. As the *Times* noted shortly before Feisal's death, in Iraq, "in practice the elections are rigged and real power is concentrated in the King."[3] As late as 1954, fully 122 of 135 seats were not contested in elections. Feisal's courtiers, the nationalist officers who had been with him since the Arab Revolt, monopolized power throughout Hashemite kingdom's existence.

After Feisal's death, neither his son Ghazi nor his grandson, the young King Feisal II, possessed even his limited personal authority. In the end, it was Nuri Said, Lawrence's wartime comrade, who came to symbolize the Hashemite monarchy he had served since the desert revolt. Appointed to his first cabinet post as internal security minister in 1922, Nuri remained a member of the Iraqi cabinet almost continuously thereafter and was eight times Iraq's prime minister. It was one of his governments that had signed the hated Anglo-Iraqi treaty of 1930, which so alienated Arab nationalists from the monarchy; Feisal's former general was also viewed by the Iraqi people as the embodiment of the hated links to London.

In the absence of political legitimacy of his own, Nuri held the Iraqi state together in the manner common in the Middle East, through repression. Opposition leaders found themselves in exile or were banned. His government employed over 20,000 secret agents, one for every Iraqi who could then read. The narrow ruling elite in Iraq was, above all, interested in safeguarding their precarious hold on power through coercion and centralized government as a tool against the fraying trends of the Shia and the Kurds and against the tendencies of all three major Iraqi communities to preserve as great a degree of autonomy as possible.

Like the British, the Iraqi government followed a strategy of centralization and repression, as if this could somehow alter the basic diverse nature of Iraq. And, as for the British, ignoring conditions on the ground doomed the enterprise to chronic instability.

In such dire circumstances, Pan-Arabism filled the niche created by the regime's artificiality. Without a national unifying common denominator for its heterogeneous population, Iraqi populists came to identify with a broader Arab identity, which while itself proved to be both artificial (various Arab groups displayed far more differences than similarities) and a political dead end, was at least founded on the reality of the common Arab experience of colonial overlordship. The British, in adopting a top-down nation-building strategy in Iraq, had created the political void that was filled by this pan-national ideal, which was the force that would destroy Feisal's bogus kingdom.

Nuri stayed in power thanks to the support of his British and American patrons. In return, he assured the continued flow of oil to their countries, and tilted toward the West against the Soviet Union in the Cold War. But in siding against General Nasser of Egypt, the hero of the Arab masses after the 1956 Suez Crisis, Nuri found himself perceived almost universally as a tool of British imperialism, standing in the way of the Arab nationalism he and Lawrence had championed in his youth.

On July 14, 1958, frail and now over 70 years old, Nuri was toppled in a coup that ended with the murder of Feisal II, the last Hashemite King of Iraq. The next day, trying to escape the city disguised as a woman, Nuri was captured by a jubilant nationalist crowd. He was shot dead and quickly buried.

The epitaph of the deeply unpopular Hashemite monarchy lay in what happened next. Nuri's corpse was exhumed the day after his murder, dragged through the streets of Baghdad, hung up, disemboweled, burned and mutilated, castrated, hacked to pieces, and beaten to a pulp. One of the groups that had orchestrated the coup was none other than a fledgling pan-Arab nationalist group, the Ba'ath Party, in which a young assassin was rising quickly through the ranks. His name was Saddam Hussein. It was the end of Lawrence's dream. The modern Iraq had been born.

*N*one of the main protagonists in the creation of modern Iraq, with one notable exception, fared well. Winston Churchill overcame the adversity of seeming irrelevance in the 1930s, eventually emerging during World War II as the indispensable man of the twentieth century. Many of the rest of the cast of characters lived frustrating lives.

After the Great War, the warrior chieftain Auda returned to his headquarters in El-Jefer. Using captured Turkish prisoners as slave labor, he built himself a palace. He died young in 1924, while he was still in his 50s.

Elected an MP in 1932, Arnold Wilson became an admirer of fascism, but joined the RAF when World War II began, serving as a tail gunner. Still an MP, Wilson was killed over Dunkirk, May 31, 1940.

Following Lloyd George's premiership, Curzon was passed over for the top job, losing out to commoner Stanley Baldwin. He died in 1925.

After Feisal's coronation, Gertrude Bell's star reached its apogee, as she was the official liaison between the British administrator, Sir Percy Cox, and the king. For a time she functioned as a virtual equal within this triumvirate. Bell was close to Feisal at first. However, her brittle manner and tendency to lecture (plus Feisal's impossible imperative to try to be seen to distance himself from the British) eventually left her with less and less of a role. Disappointed by her diminution in power in a country to which she had devoted her life, her family's immense fortune dissipated, haunted by a series of tragic love affairs, and increasingly alone, Gertrude Bell killed herself in Baghdad in 1926.

Lawrence was also not present at the final curtain call for the Hashemite dream in Iraq; he had long since fled the stage. Despite the fact that there were rumors that Churchill was gong to offer Lawrence the post of high commissioner in Egypt, replacing his one-time mentor Allenby, Lawrence instead again ran away from home.[4]

Ironically, it was at the Cairo conference, that Lawrence began toying with the idea of joining the RAF. Upon meeting its dynamic chief, Air Minster Trenchard, Lawrence, liking him, shyly asked whether he would be welcome there.

For quite some time, Lawrence had been determined to resign from his lofty perch at the right hand of Churchill. There were several immediate causes for his disillusionment. In negotiating a final settlement in Arabia with a still envious King Hussein of the Hejaz, Lawrence found working with the out-of-touch and querulous old man next to impossible. Indeed, Lawrence and the Foreign Office were soon proved to have backed the wrong long-term horse in Arabia. It was the India Office's ally Ibn Saud who was to be master of the peninsula, ousting Feisal's eldest brother and Hussein's heir as king of the Hejaz, Ali, from Arabia in 1925. To this day, the House of Saud continues to rule the modern-day Kingdom of Saudi Arabia.

Lawrence was also far from sure as to whether Abdullah, Feisal's second brother, would continue to sit quietly on the precarious throne of Jordan. Lawrence feared that Abdullah, smart but indolent, could not survive the cutthroat world of Middle Eastern politics. He was to be proved wrong here as well. Ironically, the Kingdom of Jordan is

Lawrence's sole remaining direct legacy in today's Middle East. Abdullah's great-grandson, Abdullah II, named after the founder of the dynasty, still reigns over Lawrence's curious creation.

Also Lawrence was, as ever, bored with commonplace administration at the Colonial Office. He still mocked standard operating procedures and the bureaucrats who lived and died by this dreary, routinized, creed. Churchill sensed this, later saying of Lawrence, "He was not in complete harmony with the normal."[5] Sadly, the future was with the bureaucrats. The need for knights-errant was dimming.

But there was more to Lawrence's growing desire to flee the public sphere than these immediate vexations. He was tired, desperately tired, and had begun to lose interest in the Middle East that had filled the corners of his adult life. Feeling that his debt of honor to Feisal had at last been paid, and already recoiling from the personal fame he both loved and loathed, Lawrence had no more desire to dominate the public spotlight.

It was now obvious to many that Lawrence was having a slow-motion nervous breakdown. Churchill, increasingly concerned about his great friend and ally, gives us the best sense of what his state of mind was like at the time.

"The sufferings and stresses he had undergone, both physical and psychic, during the War had left their scars and injuries upon him. These were aggravated by the distress which he felt at what he deemed the ill-usage of his Arab friends and allies to whom he had pledged the word of Britain, and the word of Lawrence. He was capable of suffering mental pain in an exaggerated degree. I am sure that the ordeal of watching the helplessness of his Arab friends in the general confusions of the Peace Conference was the main cause which decided his renunciation of all power, and so far as possible, of all interest in great public affairs."[6]

Churchill allowed Lawrence a six-month leave of absence at the end of 1921, to think things over. But his mind was made up. Although Churchill begged him to reconsider, Lawrence resigned from the Colonial Office, July 1, 1922, after only 18 months. His parting remark was that he was quit of the Arabian affair, "with clean hands."[7] This very old-fashioned, very English, desire to clean the slate, to make things right in a very personal way, had guided the whole of his postwar actions until the end.

During his years out of the public spotlight, Lawrence drifted away from both Feisal, as well as from his wartime accomplishments. Much of this had to do with the new king's diffident attitude. As Lawrence wrote philosophically to Charlotte Shaw in 1927, "Not even the nicest man on earth can feel wholly unembarrassed before a fellow to whom he owes too much. Feisal owed me Damascus first of all, and Baghdad second."[8]

Despite the hopes of many that he would reenter the public arena, Lawrence spent the rest of his life a semirecluse. In 1923, changing his name to T. E. Shaw (in honor of his close friend the playwright, George Bernard Shaw), he enlisted in the Royal Tank Corps, before eventually enlisting in the Royal Air Force, wryly noting that it was the modern equivalent of a medieval monastery. It certainly afforded a means of escape from the world that he seemed to crave.

Lawrence had once said, himself, commenting on his Anglo-Irish heritage, that he had come to the conclusion that the Irish were generally a disappointing race. "They go so far, magnificently," he noted, "and cease to grow."[9] The observation became a self-fulfilling prophesy.

The golden-haired youth of the British Empire now began a fall as stunningly sudden as that of Icarus; both had wandered too near the sun too early in their lives. Lawrence was never to reconsider the renunciation of his own fame. Reflecting on its origins in the Lowell Thomas production, he later wrote, "I wish Lowell T[homas] would die a natural death. He has, quite honestly & with the best possible motives, made life nearly impossible for me."[10]

Amazingly, the subject of Lawrence was the one point of agreement between famous antagonists Churchill and Bernard Shaw. Both viewed his withdrawal from public life with horror, seeing it as a tremendous waste for both him and England. But there was to be no second act for Lawrence; the rest of his life served merely as one long epilogue. Exhausted by his efforts to install Feisal on the Iraqi throne, dismayed by his sadomasochistic tendencies, and haunted by the celebrity he had once so craved, in 1922 Lawrence permanently withdrew from public life.

On February 26, 1935, after 12 years of relative if not total anonymity, Lawrence retired from the RAF, where he had primarily worked as a mechanic. He returned to Cloud's Hill, the cottage in Dorset that had been his home for most of his decade-plus reclusive period. Writing prophetically, and at a loss as to what to do next, he mused, "It seems as if I had finished, now."[11] He had, except for one last act of bravery.

On May 13, 1935, on his way back to his home, Cloud's Hill, returning from the Post Office, Lawrence was riding his beloved Brough motorcycle. Suddenly swerving to miss two young bicyclists who came into his view at the last minute over a slight rise in the road, Lawrence avoided killing them, but was thrown head-first over his handlebars in the effort, severely fracturing his skull.

For a week he lay unconscious in a hospital bed, as his hardened body somehow clung to life. King George V inquired after him, and the finest doctors in the land came to his bedside. But it was to no avail. Having suffered massive brain damage and never regaining consciousness, he died May 19, 1935, aged only 46.

While his death cannot be thought of as a suicide, certainly for Lawrence it was in many senses a blessed release. A distraught Bernard Shaw, who along with his wife Charlotte had bought the Brough motorcycle for Lawrence, wrote that his present "was like handing a pistol to a would-be suicide."[12]

The tributes poured in. Among them was a very public memorial service in St. Paul's Cathedral in London, where so many heroes of British history have been honored. If one gazes there at the splendid bust done of him by his friend, the sculptor Eric Kennington, one thought overcomes all else: Here lies the man who might have saved the British Empire with his vision, but chose instead to live for himself. He never lived up to the great future his contemporaries were so sure was his for the taking.

But there is a quieter, more personal memorial that signifies the man. Also done by Kennington, the old Anglo-Saxon church in Wareham, Dorset, has a splendid effigy of Lawrence, complete in Arabian regalia, laid out exactly as if he were a medieval crusader.

He would have liked that.

Chapter 11

"It is impossible for a foreigner to run another people of their own free will indefinitely, and my innings has been a fairly long one."

—Lawrence to Gilbert Clayton

Today, there is little that is tangible, with the important exception of the Kingdom of Jordan, left to remind anyone of Lawrence's legacy in the Middle East. For all his continuing appeal, with the Iraq Revolution of 1958 and the subsequent overthrow and murder of Feisal's grandson, Lawrence's relevance in the region would seem to have come to an end.

Such a view is wrong in two important senses. As this history of Lawrence's swashbuckling career makes clear, his abandonment of his philosophy for how the West should deal with the peoples of the Middle East had real-world consequences. It encouraged the rise of illiberal, illegitimate governments throughout the region in the twentieth century, regimes that were held together only through repression and the false rallying cry of war that has been the doleful narrative of the Middle East for much of the last century. It was not just Lawrence, but the Great Powers, as well as the leaders of the Middle East themselves, who intellectually misplaced the central role local political legitimacy must play in constructing a stable regional order.

More positively, Lawrence's lost philosophy may be an idea whose time has at last come. When considered in terms of the chaos in Iraq today, the conclusion is obvious: Lawrence's brilliant philosophy for working with developing peoples, sacrificed in his lifetime in order to pay his personal debts, must be rediscovered and made operational if America and the West are to avoid further disasters and if the troubled Middle East is ever to enjoy a more decent future. His ideas call to us across the chasm of time.

America's present-day difficulties in Iraq illustrate a depressing ideological sameness; Iraq is just the latest example of the failure of post–Cold War nation building. Whether we are talking about Haiti, Somalia, Bosnia, Kosovo, Afghanistan, or Iraq, one constantly runs into the same failed philosophy and the same dire results.

In the twentieth century, America intervened in Haiti over a dozen times; despite or perhaps because of this, it still remains the second-poorest country on the face of the earth, plagued by chronic political instability.

The Clinton administration left the chaos of Somalia after taking casualties over siding with one set of warlords over another. Somalia remains a black hole in the Horn of Africa, with an expanding al-Qaeda presence.

If free and fair elections were held in Bosnia today two of the three ethnic groups (the Serbs and the Croats) would vote to secede from the country. There remains no genuine political stability there, merely frozen antagonisms.

Kosovo remains a catch–22. Desperate to hand over power to the Kosovan Albanians, America and most of its western allies unilaterally accepted Kosovan independence in 2008, only to be stymied in their efforts to give the new country international legitimacy by Russian concerns about the fate of the Serb minority in the United Nations Security Council, which refused to formally recognize the new country. This has left the new state in a nebulous gray zone; all the while real power there continues to be primarily exercised by the international community.

While President Karzai of Afghanistan is finally in fact more than just the "Mayor of Kabul," his political sway surely does not extend throughout much of the fractious country. His government is unpopular and corrupt, and the Taliban are regrouping and are on the political rise.

And Iraq is . . . well, Iraq.

The lessons Lawrence taught must be remembered if this doleful record is to get any better. Top-down nation-building efforts imposed from outside, efforts that pay little more than lip service to the ideal of making locals stakeholders in the process, are doomed to failure. A top-down, foreigner-driven approach to nation building almost always ignores local cultural solutions, which are the only viable ones. The problem begins when states supported by outsiders are not held together by the basic sinews of language, geography, culture, and history.

But there can finally be a happy ending to this sad story. Embellishment aside, the core of Lawrence's intellectual brilliance is contained in what he thought and how he cooperated with the local Arabs, as much as for what he actually did. Juxtaposed in contrast, the Bush administration's follies in Iraq would serve as an almost comic foil to Lawrence's ideas, if so many lives and so much treasure had not been destroyed.

But it is not just the neoconservatives who are to blame for America's dire post–Cold War nation-building record. The Clinton administration's adventures in the Balkans and Somalia proved far from successful as well. For the bitter truth is that top-down nation-building philosophies have guided the thinking of both the Democratic and the Republican parties in the United States. In this, as in so much else, the Obama administration must break the mold, if America and the West are to have a more successful foreign policy record. For there is a different way forward. Concrete operating procedures, based on Lawrence's thought, must serve as the basis for any future effort at nation building.

Lawrence teaches us that it is critical to accurately assess the unit of politics in a failed state. He intuitively came to see that the unit of politics in Arabia was the tribe, unlike in the West. Instead of looking for Thomas Jefferson in states that have no organic tradition of democratic rule, today's Western elites must work with countries as they find them.

In the case of Iraq, the unit of politics is religious and ethnic, not that of a homogenous national people. After all the British attempts to make "Iraqis" of the locals, they still primarily identify themselves (and vote accordingly) as Shia (roughly 60 percent of the population); the formerly ruling Sunni (20 percent); and the Kurds (20 percent). The early utopian efforts by of some in the Bush Administration to ignore this reality and ape the British imperialists of yesteryear by talking of supporting "Iraqis" rather than working with the country's genuine units of politics have died down, blunted by the gloomy day-to-day political realities.

Dealing with such a complicated foreign demographic and political reality calls for adapting political structures to fit the world as it is. Far too often, outsiders try to re-establish highly centralized control in a failing state, without looking at the reasons the country fell apart in the first place. Almost always, this was due to its political system not fitting its domestic realities. In Iraq, with its deep-seated ethnic and religious divisions and complex internal politics, a far more confederal approach, one that is in tune with its three major national building blocks, suits the facts on the ground far better than the imposition of overly-centralized control, a condition that is sure to alienate these core groups, thus ensuring continuing instability. At root, if nation building is to have a chance at success, it is always primarily about local domestic politics, and not about military strategies.

To work against the grain of history and culture is to fail at nation building. Lawrence rightly understood that having Feisal's troops fight as the British did, rather than as guerrilla raiders, as they had done throughout their history, was to court disaster. Generally, to immediately and artificially impose Western standards on a failed non-Western state while disregarding its own unique culture is a doomed undertaking. For example, naïve American efforts to limit the role of Islam in the new Iraq did little more than alienate Grand Ayatollah Sistani, the key representative of the Shia Muslims, and the one man who could perhaps maintain stability among the majority Shia community, hastening America's long-hoped-for departure from Iraq.

Two rare examples of nation-building success, postwar Germany and Japan, provide more proof of the vital need to work with local cultures. Encouraging the Germans to develop a capitalistic economic structure was not difficult for a people who had, through the medieval

Hanseatic League, helped invent the system. Also, pushing for creating a federated political structure in West Germany perfectly fit the historical circumstances of a country that had not become a unified nation until very late, in 1871.

Likewise, while Douglas MacArthur may have known precious little about American political culture, he did know a great deal about the ways of his defeated Japanese foe. By preserving the Emperor and running the country as just the most recent military *shogun,* MacArthur, in the tradition of the liberalizing warlord, launched the vital agricultural and industrial reform process that set Japan on its way to becoming an economic giant. But it was the same process of renewal following military defeat that had occurred throughout Japanese history, from the time of the Tokugawa *shogunate* through the Meiji restoration. Nothing new was invented here; rather very old proclivities in German and Japanese culture were used to renew their countries.

If at all possible, it is vital not to support artificial states, which require either an immoral, expensive, and unrewarding modern form of colonialism, or outright repression to be kept on life-support.

Westerners are then forced into the two doleful choices of the Imperial trap. They either must stay on indefinitely in a failed state, artificially propping it up at great cost in blood and treasure as Arnold Wilson found to his cost, as their soldiers become regarded as occupiers rather then liberators. The other option is to cut and run, leaving the artificial country to fall apart once again.

It is local elites who must be made primary stakeholders in any successful nation-building process. Lawrence practiced this principle in Arabia by stressing that all orders given in the Arab army should come through the sherifs, and not be given by British officers.

Conversely, in disbanding the Iraqi army, Paul Bremer, a recent de facto viceroy of Iraq for President Bush, unwittingly laid the groundwork for a period in which it was the American-led coalition, rather than a fusion of American and Iraqi forces, that became responsible for the security of the country. This was perhaps America's greatest mistake in nation building in Iraq, for it meant that the West, rather than the Iraqis themselves, alone took the lead. Unwittingly, the U.S. intervention in Iraq became a quasi-colonial endeavor that kept the Iraqi people on the sidelines.

Outsiders must not pick—beyond the barest parameters of excluding from government al-Qaeda-style elements—winners and losers for other countries. The locals should make their own choices. This is not due to some misty-eyed anti-colonial view, but primarily is down to the fact that only by proceeding in such a manner can local organic legitimacy take root, an absolutely vital characteristic of any self-sustaining country.

A Republican party that was founded on the principle that domestic social engineering is a very bad idea should have known better than to try to socially engineer far-away countries of which it knew little, for instance by supporting that former neoconservative darling of the vice president's office, Ahmed Chalabi, as the faux George Washington of Iraq. For while Chalabi told the administration exactly what it wanted to hear (that despite being away from Baghdad since 1958 he somehow had a organic following in Iraq), in the end his local political support, as measured in parliamentary representation, amounted to nil. Before turning on his neocon patrons, he was just the latest in a depressingly long line of would-be American imperial stooges.

Given the hideous complexities of the process, America should engage in the arduous task of nation building only when its primary national interests are at stake. In the Great War, it was Lawrence's belief that the defeat of Turkey was possible through energizing the Arab Revolt and that this would prove greatly beneficial to a hard-pressed Britain. American efforts at nation-building ought to be discussed in similarly hardheaded terms. U.S. nation-building experiments in the 1990s displayed an undifferentiated quality in terms of American national interests, with administrations of both parties failing to make a case to the American people as to how specific interventions served U.S. interests.

The differentiation of when and where to engage in nation building, guided by national-interest calculations, will stop an overextended America from frittering away for little gain the competitive advantages that have made it the most important power in the world. It will also help American leaders to gain the necessary political support for this perilous enterprise. Sometimes the answer must be "no." As John Quincy Adams put it, in 1821, "America is the well-wisher to the freedom of all. She is guarantor of only her own."[1] Nation building is simply too complicated to be attempted more than is absolutely necessary, as in post–World War II Germany and Japan. It should be engaged in only when primary American interests are at stake.

The great eighteenth-century political thinker Edmund Burke was surely right in terms of his basic moral imperative that the central failing of most modern nation builders is that they yearn to see the world as it ought to be, rather than as it is. Only by looking at local, particularist conditions as they truly are, and not dreaming of the ease with which states with very different histories will embrace Jeffersonian ideals, can the West's modern record at nation building improve.

Above all, a tiny shred of humility is in order. In Iraq and Greater Syria, British promises to the locals were far too rosy, a critical mistake echoed by President George W. Bush's infamous "Mission Accomplished" speech. It is vital that outside powers do not over-promise what their presence in a foreign country can do for locals, who must ultimately and primarily help themselves. Lawrence historian John Mack was surely right when he said that that Lawrence's greatest gift as a leader of men was that he, "enabled others to make use of abilities they had always possessed but, until their acquaintance with him, had failed to realize."[2] That is the most, and the best, any country or person can hope to do in helping another nation find its feet.

The problems in Iraq have quieted the nation-building lobby in Washington, but only for the moment. Doubtless, soon it will rise up again, blandly claiming that it is was President Bush's incompetence, rather than their precious, not-to-be-questioned top-down nation-building strategy, that is to blame for the disaster in Iraq. This is an easy argument to make, but a false one. President Obama must not take the bait. Instead, when the moment arrives, it is up to the rest of us, guided by a rudimentary knowledge of history, to present the modern-day colonialists with a copy of *Seven Pillars of Wisdom*. Lawrence's spirit roams St. Paul's Cathedral. It is high time his ideas awoke.

Author's Note

Of course, in writing this book about Lawrence, I found only part of the man. For that is certainly the best that any biographer can do; at some level each of us remains a mystery. In Lawrence's case things are even more complicated than usual. Despite being, next to Winston Churchill, the most famous Englishman of the twentieth century, Lawrence, more than most, has remained an enigma. There have been over 30 books, several plays, an academic journal, and David Lean's magnificent if inaccurate Oscar-winning movie, and still Lawrence evades us, staying, as he liked to, just out of reach.

My own library is stuffed with a shelf-full of fine biographies of Lawrence. John Mack, Michael Yardley, Lawrence James, Malcolm Brown, and Michael Asher have all written about the man in ways that will continue to fascinate the reading public for years to come. I freely and humbly acknowledge my debt to them. Drawing on their and other fine scholarship, this book contains no new documentary revelations. However, neither, I hope, is it just another Lawrence biography going over ground already so ably covered. I hope it to be significant for two things it is not, and one thing that it may turn out to be.

The first pitfall in writing about Lawrence concerns avoiding the game of—"did he or didn't he?" The sublime British novelist, E. M.

Forster, showed that he knew his friend well when he explained that Lawrence "loved fantasy and leg-pulling and covering up his tracks, and threw a great deal of verbal dust, which bewilders the earnest researcher."[1] In the tradition of the feudal storytellers he so admired, Lawrence enjoyed turning his all-too-real adventures into stories of a legendary scale. Indeed, his masterpiece, *Seven Pillars of Wisdom,* the only modern epic, is an impressionistic and self-consciously literary retelling of the Arab Revolt. It was never supposed to be viewed as a history textbook.

Lawrence realized that by far the best way to hide the truth is through employing something just short of it. This characteristic has driven most of his biographers crazy. Some become zealous advocates of his cause, snarling at critics that his veracity is never to be doubted. Others, equally passionately, denounce him as a fraud and a congenital liar; It's almost as if his detractors do not believe that he ever left cozy Oxford for the more rigorous demands of the desert. Lawrence forces his biographers to take sides; very few people, then or now, are neutral about the man. I can imagine Lawrence, beyond the grave, enigmatically smiling at all this, as both views distort the truth to the point that he can preserve his sacred privacy.

I did not want to play his game. People who obsess about Lawrence's capacity for truthfulness in either direction miss the larger point that quite often the fact that Lawrence told less than the whole truth does not mean he generally invented his narrative either. While Lawrence delighted in sprucing up reality, he also actually did accomplish rather a lot of concrete things. For instance, there is no doubt that Lawrence bravely fought the Turks, captured vital Aqaba, and devised a brilliant strategy for victory in the Arab Revolt. I am more interested in what we know Lawrence did do, and supremely in what he thought, rather than playing this enervating parlor game.

The second pitfall of writing about Lawrence is to be so dazzled by his personality and accomplishments as to miss the essential. As his ally and admirer, Winston Churchill, put it after his death, Lawrence "held one of those master keys which unlock the doors of many kinds of treasure-houses."[2] Even at first glance, T. E. Lawrence seems particular fodder for biographers. In his time, even before he was known to the wider world, contemporaries were fascinated by him. It is easy to see why he became one of the foremost celebrities of his day, as he was a handsome, charismatic man with a record of astonishing accomplishments attained at a seemingly impossibly young age.

No one who ever met him came away without a decided opinion of the encounter. He was capable of stirring the passions of men; to this day, his defenders are as zealous as his enemies are implacable. Yet in many ways it is the ambiguities surrounding him that remain. He loved the British Empire, yet openly worked against its leaders when he felt they had betrayed both him and the Arab cause. He craved fame even as he ran away from it; privately disavowing his growing celebrity while secretly attending the public slide shows that made him famous. He was a renowned soldier who longed to be taken seriously as an artist. He was an intellectual who disdained theoretical rather than practical pursuits.

This self-contained creature was also friends with the remarkable British literary lions of his day: Rudyard Kipling, Robert Graves, E. M. Forster, and Thomas Hardy. He also had a special genius for reconciling polar opposites, inspiring great admiration and loyalty from personalities as far afield as George Bernard Shaw and Winston Churchill,

Prince Feisal of the Hejaz and King George V of Great Britain. Elites as well as the mass publics of both Britain and America adored him; yet he shied away from becoming too emotionally close to the vast majority of people he met. He did not drink and was also famously unattracted to women, who pursued him in droves in the 1920s. In the end these contradictions tore at him, causing him to flee from the public eye. He shot like a meteor across the sky, but fizzled early, just as his brightness became apparent to all.

In short, Lawrence is fascinating, even before we consider what he actually accomplished. Yet in truth, as he came to realize as he fled from his own white-hot fame, Lawrence's notoriety (and the subsequent backlash it inspired) came to obscure his real accomplishments. Somewhere along the way the startling realities of his life have become lost in the fog of modern celebrity.

In his short life Lawrence was a true Renaissance man. He was an archeologist, war photographer, mapmaker, intelligence officer, guerilla fighter, political leader, diplomat, public policy intellectual, writer, linguist, thinker, and mechanic. His interests and abilities seem designed to overwhelm the biographer from getting a sense of what in this is central, and what is interesting but less important.

Most of all, Lawrence's persona as war hero has tended to swamp everything else. For Americans, the basis of Lawrence's enduring fame is, of course, the great David Lean film *Lawrence of Arabia,* which premiered in 1962. Peter O'Toole's (a distant relative of Lawrence's) portrayal is widely considered to be one of the best acting performances in screen history. Director Lean, though playing fast and loose with the historical truth, particularly regarding what happened after the allies conquered Damascus, remained generally faithful to the spirit of *Seven*

Pillars, with gorgeous panoramic shots of the desert (with Jordan sub-stituting for Arabia) intermingling with close-ups that reveal the per-sonal struggle taking place within Lawrence himself. The beloved movie took home the Academy Award for Best Picture (and six other Oscars) and regularly shows up on lists of the best movies ever made. It is the picture most of us have of "the uncrowned king of the desert."

Viewed primarily as a warrior prince, in reality Lawrence was far more important as a thinker. This is what this book has been about. While his great deeds in Arabia remain both inspiring and a subject of controversy, his genuine intellectual gifts have been obscured. For Lawrence was far more than merely the daring, charming, swashbuck-ling guerrilla leader of the romantic Arab Revolt.

More importantly, through his direct personal experiences, Lawrence happened upon a strategy for nation building, an intellectual philosophy forged in the cauldron of the Great War, that was revolu-tionary in its time; it might well have saved the world and the Middle East a great deal of agony if it had been accepted. In the "Twenty-Seven Articles," written in August 1917 for use by British officers serving with the Bedu army, Lawrence quite brilliantly laid down a much wider philosophical basis for working with developing peoples on their way to nation building. In his later *Round Table* article, published in 1920, Lawrence applied this micro-level assessment to the world of geopolitics, dreaming of a British-dominated order, paradoxically based on a relax-ation of British control of its dominions' domestic arrangements. These largely forgotten works constitute nothing less than a new, workable blueprint for dealing with nation building in our own troubled era.

Yet it was not to be. For if this tale is Shakespearean in its cataloging of genius, heroism, betrayal, power, and friendship, one more quality must be added—that of tragedy. For in winning a throne, any throne, for Prince Feisal, Lawrence had willfully forgotten the magic that had made the Arab Revolt so special in the first place: making the locals stakeholders in the outcome, the primary actors in their own story of regeneration. Placing Feisal on the throne of Iraq followed the old model, a model that still reigns supreme in current American efforts at nation building. It is Lawrence's ideas, rather than his actions regarding Iraq in the early 1920s, that must form the basis of a more refined modern effort at nation building.

Like the administration of George W. Bush, Feisal knew nothing of the Iraqi ethnic/tribal structure, little of its history, dialect of Arabic, or economic structure. In western Arabia and Greater Syria (today's Syria, Lebanon, Israel, and Palestine) Feisal had possessed the rarest and most precious of attributes for nation building to succeed; the local legitimacy that was the cornerstone of Lawrence's philosophy. In Iraq, he was little more than a British stooge. In the moral urgency of paying his and England's debt, Lawrence let go of the one philosophy that might have made the Middle East a significantly better place.

For the best of personal reasons, Lawrence turned his back on his own intellectual creation, instead making good on his debt to his Arab wartime comrades, and single-handedly changing British imperial policy in the process. The result may have been momentarily satisfying; it proved tragically unsustainable. Today, behind all the mythology surrounding Lawrence, this most important aspect of him, the man as thinker, lies waiting to be rediscovered. This most unusual man is still worth exploring, as is the story of what happened to both him and his ideas. Indeed, what happened to Lawrence after the revolt in the desert had come to an end is a tale more fantastic and more important than anything heretofore said about the man. This is the story I hope I have told.

If Lawrence's vision of how to deal with developing peoples is a lost treasure, so the time period from 1916 to 1922 is in many ways a lost era. As for Lawrence in microcosm, it was a period when the great utopian hopes of American President Woodrow Wilson were dashed on the rocks of great power politics. The world as we know it, both for good and ill, largely grew out of the failure of the efforts to, in Wilson's words, "fight a war to end all wars." Lawrence's tale is part of the larger lost promise of his time. His story helps provide the context for the greater tragedy of the Middle East for the rest of the twentieth century; but, on a far more positive note, his forgotten ideas provide an antidote to the tragedy's continuation.

Notes

Prologue

1. *T. E. Lawrence in War & Peace: An Anthology of the Military Writings of Lawrence of Arabia,* Malcolm Brown, ed., (London: Greenhill Books, 2005), p. 54.

2. The exact quotation is, "Do not try to do too much with your own hands. Better the Arabs do it tolerably than that you do it perfectly. It is their war, and you are to help them, not to win it for them. Actually, also, under the very odd conditions of Arabia, your practical work will not be as good as, perhaps, you think it is." See ibid., pp. 144–145.

Chapter 1

1. T. E. Lawrence, *Seven Pillars of Wisdom: A Triumph* (New York: Anchor Books, 1991), p. 91.

2. Quoted in John E. Mack, *A Prince of Our Disorder: The Life of T. E. Lawrence* (Cambridge, Massachusetts: Harvard University Press, 1976), p. 38.

3. Quoted in Michael Yardley, *T. E. Lawrence: A Biography* (New York: Stein And Day, 1987), p. 48.

4. Lawrence, *Seven Pillars of Wisdom*, p. v.

5. Quoted in Michael Asher, *Lawrence: The Uncrowned King of Arabia* (London: Penguin Books, 1999), p. 321.

6. Quoted in ibid., p. 146.

7. Quoted in ibid, p. 132.

8. Quoted in ibid., p. 125.

9. Lawrence, *Seven Pillars of Wisdom*, p. 91.

10. Ibid., p. 274.

11. See Mack, p. 274.

Chapter 2

1. Lawrence, "Personal Notes on the Sherifial Family," November 26, 1916, in Malcolm Brown, *T. E. Lawrence in War & Peace; An Anthology of the Military Writings of Lawrence of Arabia,* (London: Greenhill Books, 2005), p. 80.

2. Lawrence, "The Arab Epic: Feisul's Battles in the Desert: On the Threshold of Syria," *The Times,* November 27, 1918.

3. Lawrence, "The Howeitat and Their Chiefs," July 24, 1917, in Brown, p. 133.

4. Quoted in Michael Asher, *Lawrence: The Uncrowned King of Arabia,* (London: Penguin Books, 1999), p. 243.

5. Quoted in Lawrence, "The Arab Epic."

6. Lawrence, "Extract from an Intelligence Report under Heading 'Arabia Hejaz,'" July 24, 1917, in Brown, pp. 200–201.

7. Quoted in Michael Yardley, *T. E. Lawrence: A Biography* (New York: Stein And Day, 1987), p. 105.

8. Quoted in Asher, p. 261.

9. Lawrence, "Military Notes," November 26, 1916, in Brown, p. 77.

10. Lawrence, "The Raid at Haret Ammar," October 8, 1917, in Brown, p. 149.

11. T. E. Lawrence, *Seven Pillars of Wisdom: A Triumph* (New York: Anchor Books, 1991), p. 627.

12. Quoted in Lawrence James, *The Golden Warrior: The Life and Legend of Lawrence of Arabia,* (London: Abacus, 1995), p. 188.

13. Lawrence, *Seven Pillars of Wisdom,* p. 275.

Chapter 3

1. Lawrence, "Twenty-Seven Articles," August 20, 1917, in Malcolm Brown, *T. E. Lawrence in War & Peace: An Anthology of the Military Writings of Lawrence of Arabia* (London: Greenhill Books, 2005), p. 143.

2. See Anatol Lieven and John Hulsman, *Ethical Realism: A Vision for America's Role in the World* (New York: Pantheon Books, 2006).

3. Michael Asher, *Lawrence: The Uncrowned King of Arabia* (London: Penguin Books, 1999), p. 88.

4. Lawrence, "Twenty-Seven Articles," p. 146.

5. Lawrence, "The Raid near Bir esh-Shediyah," October 21, 1917, in Brown, p. 151.

6. Lawrence, "Twenty-Seven Articles," p. 145.

7. Ibid., p. 147.

8. Quoted in Lawrence, "The Evolution of a Revolt," *The Army Quarterly,* vol. 1 (October 1920) in Brown, p. 267.

9. T. E. Lawrence, *Seven Pillars of Wisdom: A Triumph* (New York: Anchor Books, 1991), p. 62.

10. Lawrence, "Twenty-Seven Articles," p. 146.

11. T. E. Lawrence, "The Arab Epic: On the Threshold of Syria," *The Times,* November 27, 1918.

12. Lawrence, "The Evolution of a Revolt," p. 273.

13. T. E. Lawrence, "Syria: The Raw Material," March 12, 1917, in Brown, p. 108.

14. Ibid., p. 109.

15. Lawrence, "Twenty-Seven Articles," pp. 143–144.

16. Lawrence, *Seven Pillars of Wisdom,* p. 23.

17. Lawrence, "Twenty-Seven Articles," p. 143.

18. Ibid., p. 144.

19. Ibid.

20. Quoted in John E. Mack, *The Prince of our Disorder: The Life of T. E. Lawrence* (Cambridge, Massachusetts: Harvard University Press, 1976), p. 198.

21. Quoted in Lawrence James, *The Golden Warrior: The Life and Legend of Lawrence of Arabia* (London: Abacus, 2005), p. 376.

22. Lawrence, "The Changing East," *The Round Table,* September 1920, in Brown, p. 259.

23. Ibid.

24. Ibid.

Chapter 4

1. Quoted in Michael Asher, *Lawrence; The Uncrowned King of Arabia* (London: Penguin Books, 1999), p. 339.

2. Quoted in Adrian Greaves, *Lawrence of Arabia: Mirage of a Desert War* (London: Weidenfeld & Nicolson, 2007), p. 244.

3. Quoted in ibid., p. 129.

4. Quoted in Michael Yardley, *T. E. Lawrence: A Biography* (New York: Stein and Day, 1987), p. 121.

5. David Lloyd George, *Memoirs of the Peace Conference, Volume II* (New Haven: Yale University Press, 1939), p. 672.

6. Ibid.

7. T. E. Lawrence, *Seven Pillars of Wisdom: A Triumph* (New York: Anchor Books, 1991), p. 643.

8. Lawrence, "Syrian Cross-Currents," February 1, 1918, in Brown, p. 165.

9. Lawrence, *Seven Pillars of Wisdom,* p. 644.

10. Ibid., p. 649.

11. There is a good chance that Lawrence's account of his rape at Dera was basically untrue. See Asher, Yardley, and especially James.

12. Quoted in Asher, p. 339.

13. See ibid.

14. Quoted in T. E. Lawrence, "Nationalism among the Tribesmen," November 26, 1916, in Brown, p. 81.

15. Quoted in Lawrence James, *The Golden Warrior: The Life and Legend of Lawrence of Arabia* (London: Abacus, 2005), pp. 111–112.

16. Quoted in ibid., p. 310.

17. Ibid.

Chapter 5

1. T. E. Lawrence, "Reconstruction of Arabia: Memo to the Eastern Committee," November 4, 1918, in Malcolm Brown, *T. E.*

Lawrence in War & Peace: An Anthology of the Military Writings of Lawrence of Arabia (London: Greenhill Books, 2005), p. 214.

2. Lawrence, *Seven Pillars of Wisdom,* p. 651.

3. James L. Gelvin, "Demonstrating Communities in Post-Ottoman Syria," *Journal of Interdisciplinary History,* vol. 25 no.1, (Summer 1994), p. 34.

4. Ibid., p. 38.

5. Quoted in *The New York Times,* November 2, 1918.

6. Quoted in Michael Yardley, *T. E. Lawrence: A Biography* (New York: Stein and Day, 1987), p. 137.

7. David Fromkin, *A Peace to End All Peace: The Fall of the Ottoman Empire and the Creation of the Modern Middle East* (New York: Owl Books, 2001), p. 390.

8. See Wikipedia entry for "David Lloyd George."

9. Quoted in Michael Asher, *Lawrence; The Uncrowned King of Arabia* (London: Penguin Books, 1999), p. 344.

10. Quoted in Fromkin, p. 344.

11. Timothy J. Paris, "Middle East Policy after the First World War: The Lawrentian and Wilsonian Schools," *The Historical Journal,* vol. 41, no. 3, (1998), p. 778.

12. H. V. F. Winstone, *Gertrude Bell* (London: Quartet Books, 1980), pp. 248–249.

13. Gelvin, p. 42.

14. Quoted in Karl E. Meyer, "Syriana or The Godfather, Part 1," *World Policy Journal,* vol.23 no.1, (Winter 2006).

15. Quoted in Fromkin, p. 439.

16. Quoted in Brown, pp. 216–217.

Chapter 6

1. Quoted in Adrian Greaves, *Lawrence of Arabia: Mirage of a Desert War* (London: Weidenfeld & Nicolson, 2007), p. 208.

2. Quoted in ibid., p. 207.

3. Sadly many of the slides and film of the show have faded. There is no complete surviving record.

4. Quoted in Greaves, p. 216.

5. Quoted in Michael Yardley, *T. E. Lawrence: A Biography* (New York: Stein and Day, 1987), p. 157.

6. Quoted in ibid., p. 170.

7. Quoted in Michael Asher, *Lawrence; The Uncrowned King of Arabia* (London: Penguin Books, 1999), p. 354.

8. Quoted in ibid, p. 19.

9. Quoted in ibid., p. 20.

10. Quoted in Lawrence James, *The Golden Warrior: The Life and Legend of Lawrence of Arabia* (London: Abacus, 2005), p. 346.

11. Quoted in Asher, p. 37.

12. Ibid., p. 344.

Chapter 7

1. Judith S. Yaphe, "War and Occupation in Iraq: What Went Right? What Could Go Wrong?" *Middle East Journal,* vol. 57 no. 3, (Summer 2003), p. 396.

2. Wilson's tenure in Iraq came to an end in October 1920, during the waning days of the revolt.

3. David Fromkin, *A Peace to End All Peace: The Fall of the Ottoman Empire and the Creation of the Modern Middle East* (New York: Owl Books, 2001), p. 452.

4. Lawrence, "Mesopotamia: The Truth about the Campaign," *Sunday Times,* August 22, 1920.

5. Ibid.

6. Lawrence, "To the Editor of *The Times,*" *The Times,* July 22, 1920.

7. Lawrence, "France, Britain, and the Arabs," *The Observer,* August 8, 1920.

8. Ibid.

9. Lawrence, "To the Editor of *The Times.*"

10. Ibid.

11. Lawrence, "France, Britain, and the Arabs."

12. Lawrence, "To the Editor of *The Times.*"

13. Lawrence, "Mesopotamia."

14. Lawrence, "France, Britain, and the Arabs."

15. Lawrence, "To the Editor of *The Times.*"

16. Lawrence, "Mesopotamia."

17. Ibid.

18. Lawrence, "To the Editor of *The Times.*"

19. See Lawrence James, *The Golden Warrior: The Life and Legend of Lawrence of Arabia* (London: Abacus, 2005), p. 379.

Chapter 8

1. Winston Churchill, "Lawrence of Arabia," *Finest Hour,* no. 119, (Summer 2003), p. 121.

2. Quoted in David Fromkin, *A Peace to End All Peace: The Fall of the Ottoman Empire and the Creation of the Modern Middle East* (New York: Owl Books, 2001), p.556.

3. Quoted in Lawrence James, *The Golden Warrior: The Life and Legend of Lawrence of Arabia* (London: Abacus, 2005), p. 382.

4. Quoted in Timothy J. Paris, "Middle East Policy after the First World War: The Lawrentian and Wilsonian Schools," *The Historical Journal,* vol. 41, no. 3, (1998), p.779.

5. Quoted in ibid.

6. Quoted in ibid., p. 774.

7. Quoted in ibid., p. 780.

8. Quoted in ibid., p. 789.

9. Quoted in James, p. 379.

10. Quoted in Brown and Julia Cave, *A Touch Of Genius: The Life of T. E. Lawrence,* (New York: Paragon House, 1989), p. 143.

11. Quoted in Fromkin, p.499.

12. Quoted in Amal Vinogradov, "The 1920 Revolt In Iraq Reconsidered: The Role of Tribes in National Politics," *International Journal of Middle Eastern Studies,* vol. 3 no. 2, (April 1972).

13. Quoted in Michael Yardley, *T. E. Lawrence: A Biography* (New York: Stein and Day, 1987), p.173.

Chapter 9

1. Niall Ferguson, "Recovering Our Nerve," in "Iraq at the Turn," *The National Interest,* no. 76, (Summer 2004), p. 54.

2. Quoted in R. E. Cheesman, "Philby of Arabia," review of H. St. J. B. Philby, *Arabian Days: An Autobiography, The Geographical Journal,* vol. 111 no. 4/6, (April–June 1948), p. 250.

3. Quoted in John E. Mack, *A Prince of Our Disorder: The Life of T.E. Lawrence* (Cambridge, Massachusetts: Harvard University Press, 1976), p.301.

4. Quoted in David Fromkin, *A Peace to End All Peace: The Fall of the Ottoman Empire and the Creation of the Modern Middle East* (New York: Owl Books, 2001), p. 503.

5. Janet Wallach, *Desert Queen: The Extraordinary Life of Gertrude Bell: Adventurer, Adviser to Kings, Ally of Lawrence of Arabia* (New York: Anchor Books, 1999), pp. 311–312.

6. Quoted in Mack, p. 301.

7. Quoted in H. V. F. Winstone, *Gertrude Bell* (London: Quartet Books, 1980), p.235.

8. Quoted in Fromkin, p. 507.

9. Quoted in Michael Asher, *Lawrence: The Uncrowned King of Arabia* (London: Penguin Books, 1999), p. 357.

10. Quoted in Malcolm Brown, *T. E. Lawrence in War & Peace: An Anthology of the Military Writings of Lawrence of Arabia* (London: Greenhill Books, 2005), p. 249.

11. Quoted in Charles Glass, "Iraq's Founding Mother," *The Nation,* July 2, 2007.

12. Daniel Byman, "Insecuring Iraq," in "Iraq at the Turn," *The National Interest,* no. 76, (Summer 2004), p. 17.

13. Quoted in Winstone, p. 220.

14. Quoted in ibid.

Chapter 10

1. B. H. Bourdillon, "The Political Situation In Iraq," *Journal Of The British Institute of International Affairs,* vol. 3 no. 6, (November 1924), pp. 279–280.

2. Quoted in "Feisal of Iraq: Sudden Death at Berne; Son Proclaimed Ruler; Tribute by The King," *The Times,* September 9, 1933.

3. E. H. Keeling, "The New Iraq: King Feisal's Power," *The Times,* June 20, 1933.

4. See Michael Asher, *Lawrence: The Uncrowned King of Arabia* (London: Penguin Books, 1999), pp. 357–358.

5. Churchill, "Lawrence of Arabia: An Oxford Plaque; The Versatility of Genius," *The Times,* October 5, 1936.

6. Ibid.

7. Quoted in Michael Yardley, *T. E. Lawrence: A Biography* (New York: Stein And Day, 1987), p. 181.

8. Quoted in John E. Mack, *A Prince of Our Disorder: The Life of T. E. Lawrence* (Cambridge, Massachusetts: Harvard University Press, 1976), p. 302.

9. Quoted in Lawrence James, *The Golden Warrior: The Life and Legend of Lawrence of Arabia,* (London: Abacus, 1995), p. 4.

10. Quoted in Yardley, p. 195.

11. Quoted in ibid., p. 210.

12. Quoted in ibid., p. 219.

Chapter 11

1. Quoted in Scott Horton, "Blame Wilson," *ANTIWAR.com,* April 23, 2005.

2. John E. Mack, *A Prince of Our Disorder: The Life of T .E. Lawrence* (Cambridge, Massachusetts: Harvard University Press, 1976), p. xxiv.

Author's Note

1. Quoted in Lawrence James, *The Golden Warrior: The Life and Legend of Lawrence of Arabia,* (London: Abacus, 1995), p. 432.

2. Churchill, "Lawrence of Arabia: An Oxford Plaque; The Versatility of Genius," *The Times,* October 5, 1936.

Selected Bibliography

Asher, Michael. *Lawrence: The Uncrowned King of Arabia*. London: Penguin Books, 1999.

> *An interesting look at the places where Lawrence fought in Arabia and Syria; only one of 21 chapters devoted to the 1918–22 period.*

Brown, Malcolm. *T. E. Lawrence in War & Peace: An Anthology of the Military Writings of Lawrence of Arabia*. London: Greenhill Books, 2005.

> *Great in that the Twenty-seven Articles finally get their due, also good on Lawrence's letter writing campaign on Feisal's behalf after the war. Focuses on Lawrence's wartime guerrilla thinking, without seeing it as part of a larger political strategy for nation-building in general.*

Dempsey, Gary T., and Roger W. Fontaine. *Fool's Errands: America's Recent Encounters with Nation-building*. Washington, D.C.: The CATO Institute, 2001.

> *Excellent on how America's post–Cold War efforts in nation building have been disastrous, as they've all followed the same top-down, centralized formula, a formula Lawrence would recognize and despise.*

Greaves, Adrian. *Lawrence of Arabia: Mirage of a Desert War.* London: Weidenfeld & Nicolson, 2007.

> *A dual focus on an assessment of the battles Lawrence fought, as well as sifting through his untruths to look at what he actually accomplished in the desert. Nothing on the critical 1918–22 period.*

James, Lawrence. *The Golden Warrior: The Life and Legend of Lawrence of Arabia.* London: Abacus, 2005.

> *A fairly good narrative, ruined in parts by very shaky political assessments. Only two of 27 chapters devoted to Lawrence's diplomatic activities.*

Lawrence, T. E. *Seven Pillars Of Wisdom: A Triumph.* New York: Anchor Books, 1991.

> *The 1926 classic, for all its historical inaccuracies and impressionistic style, remains the only modern epic. None of it is devoted to the 1918–22 period.*

Mack, John E. *The Prince of our Disorder: The Life of T. E. Lawrence.* Cambridge, Massachusetts: Harvard University Press, 1976.

> *Still the best standard life of Lawrence, rightly winner of the Pulitzer Prize. A leading psychologist of his day writes one of the best psychological histories ever written. This, coupled with an excellent writing style and a great understanding of politics, makes this a must-read.*

Macmillan, Margaret. *Paris 1919: Six Months that Changed the World.* New York: Random House, 2001.

*Excellent on the feel and color surrounding Versailles, especially
regarding Bell, Lawrence, and Feisal. Far less good, in its overly
sunny assessment of a conference that set the stage for World War II.*

Orlans, Harold. *T. E. Lawrence: Biography of a Broken Hero.* Jefferson,
North Carolina: McFarland & Company, Inc., 2002.

*An okay effort at trying to find psychological consistency in Lawrence's
baffling later behavior. Only one chapter of 22 about Lawrence's
diplomatic dealings.*

Wallach, Janet. *Desert Queen: The Extraordinary Life of Gertrude Bell:
Adventurer, Adviser to Kings, Ally of Lawrence of Arabia.* New York:
Anchor Books, 1999.

*Though the writing sometimes gets in the way, a great story, and, at
present, the definitive read on Gertrude Bell. Great asides about
Lawrence, Feisal, and how it all went wrong in Baghdad.*

Yardley, Michael. *T. E. Lawrence: A Biography.* New York: Stein and
Day, 1987.

*Good on the myth-making surrounding Lawrence. Only two of 19
chapters devoted to his diplomatic period.*

Index